# THE BIG DIG

## THE MIRACLE OF WASCANA CENTRE

### BOB HUGHES

Leader-Post

# THE BIG DIG
## by Bob Hughes

Second Printing – November 2004

Copyright@2004 by
Leader-Post Ltd.
1964 Park Street
P.O. Box 2020
Regina, Saskatchewan Canada  S4P 3G4

All rights reserved. Except for short passages for reviews, no part of this book may be reproduced, stored in a retrieval system or transmitted in any form or by any means, electronic, mechanical, photocopying, recording, or otherwise without the prior written permission of the publisher.

## CANADIAN CATALOGUING IN PUBLICATION DATA

Hughes, Bob, 1944 –

    The big dig : the miracle of Wascana Centre / Bob Hughes ; Margo Embury, editor.

ISBN 1-897010-06-0

    1. Wascana Centre (Regina, Sask.)  2. Wascana lake (Regina, Sask.)  3. Urban renewal – Saskatchewan – Regina.  I. Embury, Margo, 1943–  II. Title.

FC3546.52.H83 2004           333.78'3152'09712445         C2004-906192-5

Cover Design by
Brian Danchuk, Brian Danchuk Design

Front cover photo by Bryan Schlosser

Project Coordinator
Dan Marce, Publishing Solutions, a division of PrintWest Communications Ltd.

Formatting and page design by
Iona Glabus, Centax Books

Printed and Produced in Canada by
Centax Books, a division of PrintWest Communications Ltd.
Publishing Director and Editor – Margo Embury
1150 Eighth Avenue, Regina, Saskatchewan, Canada S4R 1C9
(306) 525-2304                     Fax (306) 757-2439
E-mail: centax@printwest.com         www.centaxbooks.com

# TABLE OF CONTENTS

| | |
|---|---|
| DEDICATION | 4 |
| COMMUNITY PARTNERS | 5 |
| ACKNOWLEDGEMENTS | 6 |
| AUTHOR'S NOTE | 7 |
| FOREWORD | 11 |
| INTRODUCTION | 15 |
| CHAPTER 1 – History | 18 |
| CHAPTER 2 – The Dig – 1931 | 26 |
| CHAPTER 3 – "Got the Ball Rolling" | 30 |
| CHAPTER 4 – October 2003 – The Beginning | 32 |
| CHAPTER 5 – November & December 2003 | 38 |
| CHAPTER 6 – January 2004 | 42 |
| CHAPTER 7 – In the Pit | 48 |
| CHAPTER 8 – February 2004 | 58 |
| CHAPTER 9 – March 2004 | 68 |
| CHAPTER 10 – The Guy in the Pit | 80 |
| CHAPTER 11 – Looking Back | 84 |
| CHAPTER 12 – Memories | 94 |
| CHAPTER 13 – In the End, Regina Won | 114 |
| THE BIG DIG – Facts & Figures | 119 |
| 1931 DIG – Facts & Figures | 124 |
| AUTHOR BIOGRAPHY | 127 |

# DEDICATION

This book is dedicated to my mother and father,
Bob and Beth Hughes,
who belonged to the Regina Rowing Club
and introduced me to the joys of Wascana Park
and swimming in Wascana Lake.

# COMMUNITY PARTNERS

The Raise-a-Reader Campaign and The Leader-Post Carrier Foundation thank the following community partners whose contributions have helped make possible the publication of this book:

Broda Construction Inc.
Clifton Associates Ltd.
Dominion Construction Inc.
Kramer Ltd.
Leader-Post Ltd.
PrintWest Communications Ltd.
Wascana Centre Authority

photo by Bryan Schlosser

*The Big Dig in full throttle*

# Making the Book

When The Big Dig wrapped up in March, and the last of Broda Construction's equipment had left the bottom of Wascana Lake and the water was pouring in, there was a huge letdown. This whole project had been such a rush for the people of Regina and surrounding area who came on a daily basis to watch the work being done.

The obvious question when it was over was, "Now what?"

Nobody seemed to want to let it go, so captivating was the whole experience. There were many inquiries from people who wondered if a book would be written on The Big Dig. *The Leader-Post* decided it would indeed be appropriate if a book was written which told the story of not only The Big Dig but also of Wascana Centre. Long-time *Leader-Post* columnist Bob Hughes went to work and wrote the book. Printwest was brought in as the publisher with Dan Marce heading up its side. It also was decided that all proceeds from the book would go the Raise-a-Reader campaign and the Leader-Post Carrier Foundation.

Hughes and Marce spent endless hours searching for old photographs and pouring over photographs from The Big Dig. They estimate they must have looked at well over 6,000 photographs. Hughes spent considerable time researching the history of the park and talking to people who had used it for most of their lives. The photographers – especially the Leader-Post's Roy Antal, Don Healy and Bryan Schlosser – went beyond the call of duty in coming up with wonderful photographs.

The result is The Big Dig.

# ACKNOWLEDGEMENTS

| | | |
|---|---|---|
| Roy Antal | Don Healy | Bob Newton |
| Mark Behrns | Brenda Indzeoski | Tim Novak |
| Will Chabun | Carey Isaak | Dan Reban |
| City of Regina Archives | Lorne and Sheila Kirzinger | Regina Rowing Club |
| Rusty Clunie | Leader-Post Ltd. | Saskatchewan Archives Board |
| Pam Cowan | Carla Machuk | Bryan Schlosser |
| Ken Dockham | Dan Marce | Wayne Standon |
| Margo Embury | Sue Marshall | Wascana Centre Authority |
| Iona Glabus | Ken McMurchy | |

# Author's Note

I remember it, if somewhat vaguely. I remember the dock, the people and the water. The noise. Jumping into the water. And swimming. I could not have been much more than four years old. I remember the park and the picnics, the games we played as children, hide and seek or tag, or just running around.

*Bob Hughes age 4, standing on the dock at Wascana Lake*

*Saskatchewan History and Folklore Society – Everett Baker Collection*
*Regina Rowing Club in the 1940s*

It would have been in the late 1940s. My father, Bob, known as Sailor Bob, was an active member of the Regina Rowing Club and he and my mother, Beth, who was a nurse, were down there all the time. The club was located on the north shore of Wascana Lake. They would take me with them, and that is how I got to know Wascana Park and the lake itself. And while I may not have appreciated it then, that was when I discovered the wonders of this most amazing man-made park and body of water anywhere in North America – right smack in the middle of a city. Our city. Regina. The Queen City of the Prairies.

My love affair with Wascana Park has only grown stronger as time and years have passed. As I became a young man and began work at the *Leader-Post*, I spent many a weekday afternoon playing touch football in Wascana Park. When the days were boring and there was nothing else to do, or I was writing a letter to my parents, who by then were living in Toronto, I would go over to the museum in the park, just a block away from my boarding house at 2341 McIntyre Street, and enjoy the peace and quiet of the place. I could, and did, spend hours there.

*Hughes' family photo*
*Regina Rowing Team, 1940s, Bob Hughes Sr. (Sailor Bob) at right*

*Hughes' family photo*

*Regina Rowing Team, 1940s*

I have always enjoyed walks and bike rides through the park; it was also a nice place to take a pretty girl on a Friday night.

*photo by Bryan Schlosser*

*The park is for kids*

But I never enjoyed Wascana Centre as much as I did when my two boys, Geoffrey and Ryan, were young. Every Sunday morning I would take them on lengthy walks through the park, walks that would start at our house in the 3400 block of Angus Street, wrap around the full circle of the lake, and then, if it was an especially nice morning, we would reverse our path and redo the whole thing.

Even now, the wonders of Wascana Centre take me there for times of relaxation, relief, or just to sit on a park bench among the trees and enjoy the moment. To this very day it remains a great place to go for a long walk. You would never guess you were in the centre of a major Canadian city. You can leave the buzz of your workplace and, within minutes, find yourself in the midst of tall trees, under a blue sky, as if you had snapped your fingers and had been transported to Waskesiu.

Wascana Centre has grown so much over the decades. It provides many options for the people of Regina. It is used by cultural groups for summer picnics, family reunions, class excursions, athletic competitions as big as the Canada Summer Games and as colourful as the Dragon Boat Races, community celebrations such as Waskimo and Buffalo Days. It serves up an endless menu of relaxation and fun.

photos courtesy of Wascana Centre Authority

*Waskimo is an annual winter festival*

photo by Bryan Schlosser

*Dragon Boat Races – grade 7 and 8 students from Lakeview School*

Thankfully, we recognize that not only do we have a jewel in the centre of town, but it also must be polished and cared for. For years, there had been a push on to get Wascana Lake deepened, but it was too often dismissed as being too expensive. But what would be Regina be without Wascana Lake and Wascana Centre? And what would Wascana Centre be without the lake?

When that ambitious $18-million project to deepen the lake began in the winter of 2003, it took on something nobody had expected would happen. It became the city's top tourist site, for both Reginans and visitors to the city.

*photo by Ann Wood*

*On the coldest days, people came to watch The Big Dig*

Every single day, hundreds of people would go through the park to stop and watch the amazing procession of men and heavy equipment peeling the bottom off the lake. The workers themselves became celebrities, with people waving at them, holding up signs on the bridges, saluting them or taking them food. The work went on 24 hours a day, seven days a week and when it was finished, the citizens of Regina had developed a new pride in their newly enhanced park. More and more people are now visiting it every day.

I have been caught up in few events as much as I was in the deepening of Wascana Lake. Unless I was out of town, there was not a day that went by when I did not drive through the park. Sometimes, I would go down in The Pit and the view from there, looking up from the bottom, up to the shores, was enough to take my breath away. Standing next to the big hoes and the massive rock trucks gave me a true appreciation of how huge this equipment really was.

I also came to understand how talented the people from Clifton Associates, Dominion Construction and Broda Construction really were, and how dedicated and excited they were to be a part of this project.

*photo by Adrien Bolen*

*Earthmoving machines in action*

The Big Dig was one of the great chapters in Regina's history for so many reasons. But the most fundamental reason was that it once again showed that, when determined, there are very few things the City of Regina cannot accomplish.

Bob Hughes, Regina
September 2004

# FOREWORD

*Saskatchewan History and Folklore Society – Everett Baker Collection*

*The legislative gardens have always been stunning*

It was the last Sunday in June in 2004. Finally, summer had arrived, late, but finally dislodging the chilly temperatures, the cool winds, the clouds that had delivered rain virtually all spring. A soft, warm breeze felt good. The sky, that inimitable Saskatchewan blue, had popcorn puffs of cloud gliding across.

It was the day before the federal election, but politics and this kind of day did not go hand in hand. As I drove past Wascana Centre, the view was spectacular.

The rains had turned the lawns and the trees to the deepest shades of green that I can remember. The flowers in the long strip leading from the lakeshore up toward the Legislative Building were reaching for the sun and their colours were dazzling. The deep waters of Wascana Lake shimmered in the sunlight.

And as I watched all of this unfolding, I thought, "This is what it was all intended to be." I am talking of what was happening in Wascana Centre on this day, and would be going on in this place from now until eternity. I can remember, as a child, swimming off the dock of the Regina Rowing Club where my mother and father were members. I can remember all of the pleasures this place in the sun had provided for the people of Regina. And, on this last Sunday in June, it had taken on a new life, a rebirth.

This is what the park was intended to be when our forefathers conceived the idea – carved out a lake from prairie soil and planted a forest so many decades ago.

Wascana Centre reached a new maturity in 2004. And you had only to be there on that first nice day of summer, on that last Sunday in June, to see it, feel it, experience it.

*Saskatchewan Archives – RA15776*

*Wascana dock in years long gone*

A small sailboat, with brightly coloured sails, left a small crease in the dark waters as it skimmed across the lake at the south end, not far from the newly constructed Pine Island.

Canoes carried people on family outings, the paddles cutting into the water as they hugged the shoreline on the east side, just down from Willow Island. A band of kayaks huddled together near Spruce Island, discussing, no doubt, where next on the lake they would go. They sat atop the deepest part of the lake, a depth of about 8 metres, a fish hole is what it is called, the rest of the lake being about 5 to 6 metres deep.

*photo by Don Healy*
*Sailing instructor Mark Boots (left)*

*photo by Don Healy*
*Ready for competition on the lake*

The rowers were knifing through the water, the sculls moving swiftly, the oars dropping in unison, no weeds to catch and torment them. All that was gone. The water was now free of the weeds that had threatened to turn the lake into nothing more than a marsh.

Around the shoreline was a moving chain of humanity, linked only by their discovery of the joy of using Canada's most celebrated urban park in the way it was always intended to be used. Everywhere you looked, people were walking, jogging, riding bikes, pushing baby carriages. It was an endless procession of smiling families, playful children, contented senior citizens, and just plain people. Some sat on the benches near the shore, just relaxing, talking and taking it all in.

Inside the park, on the south side near the totem pole, the picnic tables were filled with coolers and paper plates, the trappings of a wonderful way to spend a Sunday afternoon. One family had set up a badminton net and the kids were smacking the bird back and forth. Their laughter carried through the tall pines. White strands of smoke lazily floated into the sky from the barbecues, the hamburgers and wieners tenderly being turned over by ladies in shorts and tee shirts. The kids could smell them cooking and soon they would be over, eagerly holding the empty buns in their outstretched hands.

Everywhere in the park there was activity. The museum on the northwest border of the park welcomed visitors to stroll its fascinating corridors. The Science Centre on the northeast side, where the Power Plant once stood, invited participation in its ever-changing exhibits. Everywhere, people gathered to explore, to watch, to just enjoy.

As I was watching all of this on that gentle June afternoon, I could think only that this was what Wascana Centre was intended to be. A gathering spot for people to enjoy in the middle of their city. A place that stands in stark, bold and engaging contrast to the daily grind of city life. The park provides ready access to the refreshing revitalization of nature.

The Big Dig of the winter of 2004 had not only saved the lake from evaporating into thin air, leaving only a useless marsh; it had not only put into motion the enhancement of the park, making it even more beautiful and more enjoyable; it also had opened the door of discovery for Reginans and for those who visit our city.

Suddenly, people who had never really used the park were drawn to it out of curiosity. And once they got there, they felt a deep sense of pride in what this city was capable of and what it offered right at our front door. Throughout the winter, thousands of people had visited the park to watch the huge machinery at work, digging out the bottom of the lake. It was as fascinating to watch as it was incredible. Millions of dollars worth of machines worked around the clock to get the job done.

It became one of the biggest stories in Regina's history. One that, as it unfolded, was true to the city's history, which is the ongoing saga of a people who have maintained the principles of those who first settled in Regina. That being, if you want something done, you find a way to do it yourself. And, so, Regina did just that in the winter of 2004.

This book is the story of Wascana Centre, its history, the memories that have flowed from the people who have used it for so many years, and, of course, The Big Dig.

*photo by Roy Antal*

*Biking around the new lake*

# Wascana Lake Urban Revitalization Project

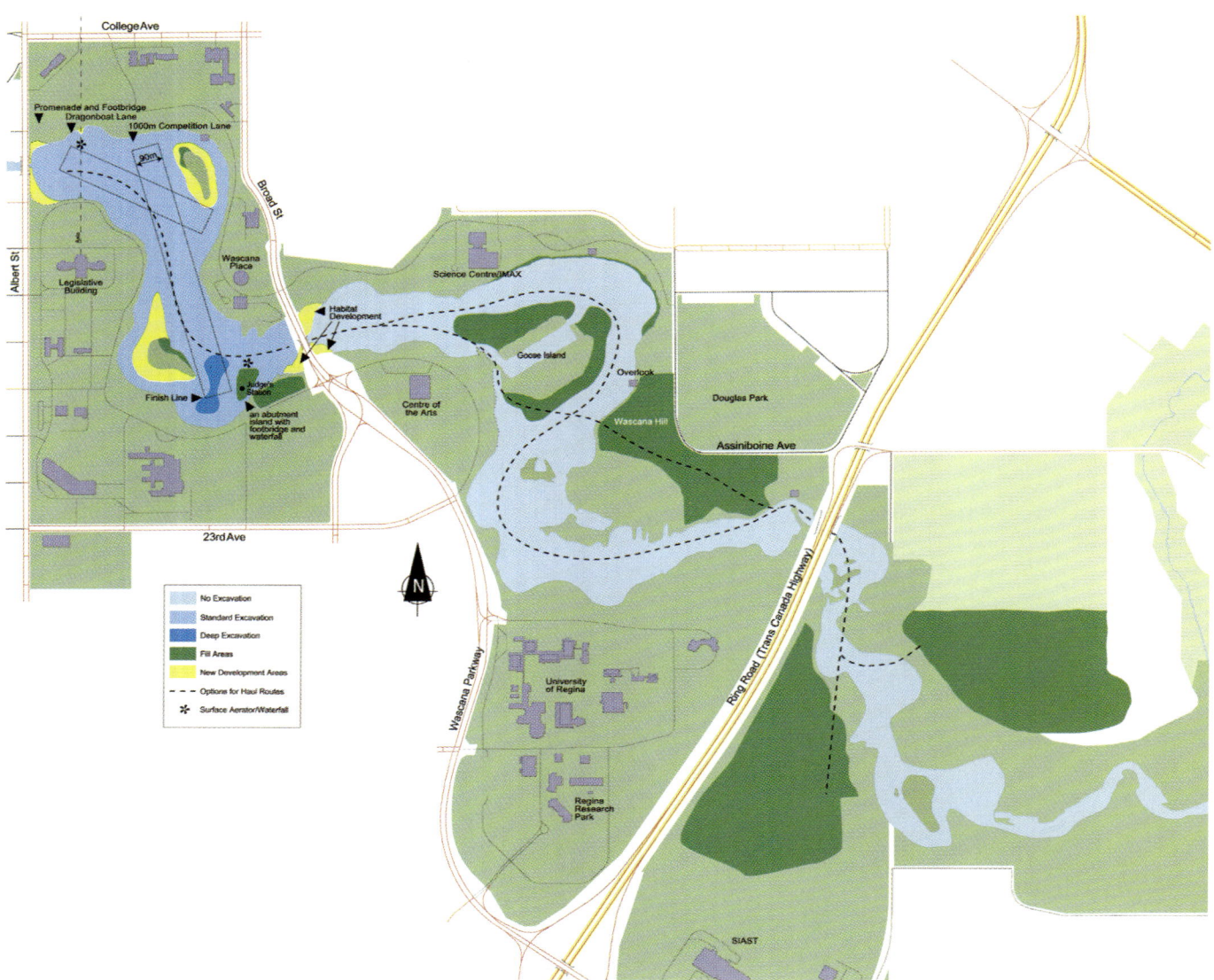

*Map courtesy of Wascana Centre Authority*

# Introduction

As I write this, we are coming out of the long May weekend in the year 2004. It is a lousy weekend for weather. There are great banks of dark clouds clinging to the rooftops of the city, pelting Regina with slivers of water that shine silver in the failing light. And a clinging cold goes to the bones and stays there, an unwelcome intruder.

In the centre of town, the rain is splashing down on Wascana Lake and the wind, with its usual prairie muscle, is forming waves on the water that spills into it from Wascana Creek. The level of the lake is rising swiftly as the heaviest rain of the spring descends. The park itself is taking on a deeper shade of green, leaves beginning to sprout from the branches that spent the winter as grey skeletons. The grass is turning emerald, and soon everything will be full of the colours of summer. On this day in late May, the park is not filled with the streams of visitors who have come every winter and early spring weekend as if on some sort of pilgrimage. It is too wet and too chilly, a day to stay inside and light a fire, read or watch a movie. And, so, they have.

The park sits in its silence in the middle of one of the most incredible cities in the world. Regina. The Queen City of the Prairies. Pile of Bones. The little town that not only could, but did. How can you not help but love this place? It is a city that from the very beginning had the imagination of 1,000 children, the strength of a mountain, the nerve of Houdini, the stamina of a farmer at harvest, the dedication of a heart surgeon. How else can you explain, describe, comprehend, the turning of all these acres of dirt and dust and scrub grass and loneliness and nothingness into a place that has become one of the great cities in the country?

Baby, you've come a long way!

*photo courtesy of Stan Krause*

*Even when there were no trees, there was still a place for people to go and enjoy themselves*

I can remember one night over dinner in our house when the great amateur football coach Gordon Currie and his wife, Shirley, were guests. We talked of a lot of things that lazy evening and, for whatever reason, why this place on the map was chosen to be the location for Regina. Why couldn't our forefathers have settled on Fort Qu'Appelle or Lumsden, or somewhere in a valley, or someplace where there were trees, and perhaps even a river? Why would they set up their tents on land that was flat and boring and empty, and had only the wind and blowing dust as constant companions? They called this place Pile of Bones for good reason. That is about all that was here – piles of buffalo bones.

I said to Gord Currie that I had seen ancient photographs of Regina in its beginnings, when along Albert Street there were only a couple of houses and another couple of houses on McCallum Avenue. They were large homes, and they are still standing, but what struck me most about them was their isolation. They stood alone in empty fields. There was not a single tree anywhere. Not one. Just emptiness.

*Saskatchewan Archives R-D1884*

*Albert Street near the Legislative Building – 1912 – trolley car at left; street paving in process*

Why here for Regina? "A lot of it likely had to do with the railway," said Currie. And, of course, he was right. The railways decided where a lot of towns and cities would be located, which explains why many Saskatchewan towns are named after railwaymen.

Regina had a harsh beginning but, as it would turn out, the toughness of the people transformed this empty little prairie outpost into a prairie oasis that today is a candidate for anybody's postcard.

There were many ingredients that went into the recipe. But two stand out as essential to its success.

One was the decision to start planting trees. This may well bring laughter from those who have spent their lives in Vancouver or Toronto. Not in Regina. In Regina, anything the city has is because its citizens put it there and that commands an even deeper sense of pride in the city. There wasn't a single tree in sight when Regina was born. Every tree was hand-planted. And now there of thousands of them, throwing themselves into the sky in the older neighbourhoods, shading the magnificent homes that form the neighbourhoods that were the beginnings of Regina. In the years to come, thousands more will spring from the ground in our new developments.

Then, there was the incredibly foresightful decision to bring from the flat empty land a park, and a lake, right in the middle of the city. This park has become Wascana Centre, managed by the Wascana Centre Authority, owned by the people of Saskatchewan.

*Saskatchewan Archives Board – R-A24145*
*Wascana Lake and Rotary Park in the early days*

*Saskatchewan Archives Board – R-B9680*
*Swimmers enjoying Wascana Lake – 1940s*

Wascana Centre has long been considered the "jewel" of Regina. It is one of the very few significant parks that sits in the middle of a Canadian city.

And in the winter of 2003-2004, it took on an even prettier face. In perhaps the most ambitious project ever accomplished in Wascana Centre, and perhaps even in the whole city, dozens of pieces of huge machinery and hundreds of men went onto the lake bed and dug it out. And when the spring runoff began, and the water poured into the new deep lake bed, Wascana Lake had a fresh look – better and more beautiful than before.

It was an $18-million job, with funding from three levels of government, federal, provincial and city. And it took the combined efforts and imagination of three outstanding Saskatchewan companies to pull it off – Clifton Associates of Regina, Dominion Construction of Regina and Broda Construction of Prince Albert. Once all of the other enhancements are completed – the promenade, the waterfall, the new island – the jewel of the City of Regina will be shining even brighter than before.

It wasn't always that way.

# Chapter 1 – History

Part of the beauty of Wascana Centre is its conception, the vision from which it came. It was not a natural formation like many of the great parks in this country. Prince Albert National Park was a logical place for a park. It had thousands of acres of rich forest, rivers and rocky streams, lakes so clear you could see the bottom, and weather that brought forth the best in each season. Cypress Hills was a contrasting display of nature presenting itself in arresting beauty. It had rolling plains of long grass, swaying like ocean waves, and a dramatic escarpment that displayed great lodgepole pines and cliffs in stunning contrast with the golden flowing land below.

Wascana Centre and, by inclusion, Wascana Lake had none of that. Why, there wasn't even a lake in the beginning. In the beginning, there was only a tabletop expanse of dirt that seemed to drop off the curve of the earth. There were no trees. There was only flat land that went on as far as the eye could see. Early photographs of the Legislative Building show a far different story from what we see today. There was only a huge building looming large over the lake, naked against the sky. This was the most unlikely place to build a park. When the wind howled, the sky would go dark from the dust being carried across the prairie to some distant resting place. Before the park, there was only dry prairie.

*photo courtesy of City of Regina Archives RPL-A-755*

*Boxcars on railway line in front of Legislative Building delivered limestone for its construction – ca. 1910*

It was the government which provided the beginnings of Wascana Centre. In the 1880s, before there was even a province of Saskatchewan, there were only a couple of wells in Regina to augment the supply of water that was available from a creek. The federal government and the CPR built an earth dam across Wascana Creek, just west of the present Albert Street Bridge. This resulted in the creation of a water reservoir of about 65 hectares, with an average depth of 1.5 metres. Its primary purpose was to provide water for stock. But the people of the city quickly saw it as an opportunity to go sailing or canoeing without having to leave the city. They had a lake.

Not until the early 1900s did any building rise above the lake. The City of Regina emerged from its humble beginnings as the hamlet of Pile of Bones, named because of all of the buffalo bones found in the vicinity. It became the City of Regina in 1903, with a population of 3,000. In 1905, the Province of Saskatchewan was established and Regina was officially declared the capital. A grand new city hall was built in 1908, on the site where the Galleria now sits.

*photo courtesy of City of Regina Archives RPL-A-422*

*Reservoir Dam and first Albert Street Bridge ca. 1900*

*Saskatchewan Archives R-A3734-2*

*Row, row, row your boat . . .*

The Province of Saskatchewan emerged from the Assiniboia area of the Northwest Territories and operated out of territorial buildings which stand on the north side of Dewdney Avenue between Athol and Montague Streets. The new provincial government under Premier Walter Scott decided to build a new Legislative Building, but there wasn't enough room to build one where the territorial buildings were. Other sites were considered. One was in Victoria Park. Another was on the north side of Wascana Lake. One more site was considered and it was ultimately chosen – the south side of the reservoir. It got the nod because of its elevation and the view it offered of the city.

Before the building was constructed, the government appointed a Montreal landscape architect named Frederick Todd to put together plans for the project. The people of those days possessed the kind of vision from which the citizens of today continue to reap the benefits. Although much of Todd's plan was not followed, one major suggestion was taken seriously. Had it not been, Wascana Centre may never have become what it did become. He saw the need for trees and this proposal was followed closely. The cost of transplanting trees would be very expensive, so Todd suggested that a large quantity of seedling plants, to be used for transplanting, be purchased and grown for a year or two on favourable soil in the Regina area.

*Saskatchewan Archives R-B 1499*

*A gathering place for people, always the story of Wascana Centre*

*photo courtesy of City of Regina Archives A-1536*

*Old Albert Street Bridge – 1915 flood*

By late spring of 1913, about 11,000 trees and shrubs had been planted on the grounds surrounding the Legislative Building and the beginnings of the park had taken root. It was only the start.

The north side of the lake was not established as a park until 1906, but the idea to use it as such was born with the birth of the city in 1903.

From almost the very beginnings of Regina, Wascana Park was not intended to be used for commercial purposes. But there was a moment in its history when it also bent to the call of capitalism. In 1913, city council leased the northwest corner of Albert Street and College Avenue to the Grand Trunk Railway to build a big hotel, which would be called the Chateau Qu'Appelle. The steel framework for the hotel was completed by the time World War 1 was declared and the skeleton stood until 1920, when it was torn down after the Grand Trunk declared bankruptcy. The area was restored to park use. The foundations for the Chateau Qu'Appelle remain in place to this very day, just north of the Royal Saskatchewan Museum. There are still those who maintain that a grand hotel in the park would draw more tourists to Wascana Centre and enhance its appeal even more. Others maintain that the park's heritage and integrity must be maintained.

*illustration by Bill Argan*

*Chateau Qu'Appelle Hotel – the hotel that never was . . .*

*Saskatchewan Archives R-B9548*

*The north shore of Wascana Lake as seen from the top of the Legislative Building*

As time went on, an education facility was developed along College Avenue, on the north side of the lake, which would ultimately lead to the birth of the University of Regina. The government of the day was continually busying itself with plans and studies to grow Wascana Park. In the 1930s, the government hired Thomas Mawson and Son, City Planners of London, England, who had offices in Vancouver. Their assignment? "To improve without disturbing." Mawson's plans centred on the legislative grounds but included the north side of the lake on both sides of Broad Street. Mostly, he will be remembered for continuing to develop the areas around the lake, especially the landscaping around the Legislative Building.

In the early 1960s, the University of Saskatchewan in Saskatoon decided to set up a satellite campus in Regina, and the area along the south side of College Avenue, stretching from Broad Street to Cornwall, was used as classrooms for students. This also led to the ultimate formation of the University of Regina. It became obvious that Regina was indeed a "chosen" city. Providentially, there were huge parcels of land available within the city that could be used as the site for the campus of the University of Regina, land that stretched out along the southeastern portion of the Hillsdale area, alongside what is now the Ring Road.

It also became obvious at this time that Wascana Park was too precious a jewel for the City of Regina to leave without any formal protection, or organization. From that observation came the formation of the Wascana Centre Authority. In April of 1962, the Wascana Centre Act was passed by the Provincial Legislature. The preamble to the act laid down the wider purposes of Wascana Centre. It read, in part, "It is deemed expedient and desirable that an area surrounding Wascana Lake in the City of Regina, to be known as Wascana Centre, be devoted to the development of the seat of government, the enlargement of educational opportunities, the advancement of the cultural arts and the improvement of recreational facilities." A 1989 amendment to the act spelled out one further aim – conservation of the environment.

Perhaps, the need for the creation of the Wascana Centre Authority and the Wascana Centre Act came in 1961 when there was another push to develop a further plan for the creation of the new University of Regina campus. The government went searching for a world-renowned planner, and a list of 11 planners was submitted. In June of 1961, the man chosen to be the master planner for the new campus was Minoru Yamasaki of Birmingham, Michigan. Two months later, his role was expanded when he was named architect/planner for the proposed Wascana Centre. His appointment was perhaps the most dramatic step in the development of the Centre because it allowed planning for the whole Wascana Centre to proceed hand in hand with the development of the university. It was a big stretch, but Yamasaki had the genius to pull it off.

What Yamasaki brought to Regina was the fresh view of an outsider, someone who was not familiar with the city, who was seeing it for the first time, and who, because of that, saw such wonders he could hardly contain his excitement.

*Minoru Yamasaki is welcomed by Hon. Alan Blakeney, Minister of Education, 1962*

A big headline in the *Leader-Post* read, "Yamasaki claims Wascana Centre's future unequalled." He was quoted, "Wascana is going to make Regina one of the greatest cities in the world. There won't be a centre equal to this in the world."

His plan called for both shores of Wascana Lake, from Albert Street to the Ring Road, to be developed into a parkland sanctuary for government, culture, tourists and birds. So simple. So concise. And so brilliant.

There have been so many benchmarks since Wascana Centre had its humble beginnings at the turn of the Twentieth Century. But, always, it has maintained its role as a place for people.

*As Wascana Centre grew, so did the city*

*Saskatchewan Archives R-A3739-1*

*Sailboats sit in silence and a few homes are visible on Albert Street in a time long, long ago*

Photos, old photos, tell an amazing story of Wascana Centre's growth. There is a picture of the Regina Boat Club on the north shore of the lake in 1900, a lonely white sentinel standing in treeless surroundings. There is a 1910 photo of canoes traveling east on the lake with the Legislative Building in the background. There is a 1945 photo of the north side swimming pool and, of course, photos of the Canada geese in their lake habitat. In 1956, the eastern portion of the lake was declared a Federal Migratory Bird Sanctuary, where over 200 pairs of breeding Canada geese nest and more than 115 species of birds stop over during migration.

*Saskatchewan Archives R-A6585-1*

*The north shore of Wascana Lake in the early days*

The park has matured remarkably from the days when it was nothing but vast prairie set in the middle of nowhere. There are now parks within the park, places for all ages to go and utilize.

One such is Candy Cane Park. Originally, it was named Family Amusement Park. It was built in 1979 during the International Year of the Child. Located on the east side of the centre, just off the bend in the lake, in the shadows of the Saskatchewan Science Centre, it is a place for children to play. There are also a number of picnic sites nearby.

There is Douglas Park. First developed in 1964, it is home to tennis courts, cricket pitches, ball diamonds, football and soccer fields and, of course, a track and field area that is undergoing enhancements for the 2005 Canada Summer Games. At the west end of Douglas Park is a hill that offers a spectacular view of Regina.

There is Lakeshore Park. It's the second oldest park in Wascana Centre and easily one of the most popular picnic areas. In August of 1964, four barbecues were built. They proved to be so popular that 12 picnic sites were developed with charcoal barbecues, two to three picnic tables and benches at each site. The centrepiece is the Kwakiutl Totem Pole, donated to the people of Saskatchewan by the First Nations Peoples of British Columbia to celebrate British Columbia's 100th anniversary. There is also the Boy Scout Monument and, further east, the Surveyor's Monument.

There is Wascana Park. Located on the north shore of the lake, these 44 acres comprise the first park developed along the creek. Within this area are such well-known features as the Royal Saskatchewan Museum, Wascana Bandstand, Wascana Pool and Speakers' Corner.

And there is Waterfowl Park. This is a 223-hectare marshland devoted to the protection of birds. Its existence goes back to 1913 when somebody had the foresight to establish the Wascana Game Preserve. Part of the preserve later became the Wascana Bird Sanctuary and the Regina Waterfowl Park.

The main body of the lake also contains man-made islands. They are Willow Island, Spruce Island and Pine Island. Willow and Spruce were built in 1931, during the depression, when over 2,000 men went into the drained lake bottom and deepened it in one of the most amazing projects ever undertaken in this city. Much of the dirt removed was used to form Willow and Spruce Islands. Pine Island was an offspring of The Big Dig of 2004. It was cut away from the south shoreline where the old Broad Street Bridge once stood.

It has taken 100 years for Wascana Centre to get to where it is today. But it has been a trip well worth while. And one that is far from over.

photo courtesy of Saskatchewan Property Management Corporation

*It's only just begun . . .*

# Chapter 2  The Dig – 1931

The sun was relentless. It started early in the morning and by noon it had baked the land. The ground, so dry from no rain, cracked open, horrible zigzags of broken land as far as the eye could see. When the wind came up, it lifted and carried the dust. The air turned black with clouds of dirt that spread across the horizon. These were the times of drought, the times of the Great Depression, and Saskatchewan was slowly but surely having the life squeezed out of it.

The Depression produced unemployment. Families were forced to give up their homes. Farms stood empty, lifeless. The land where crops once flourished now had only sparse wheat stubble left in the ground. In some places, where the land was really dry and where the wind seemed to never tire, dirt was piled up against farm buildings the way snow would drift onto them in winter.

There was an immense feeling of hopelessness as first hundreds and then thousands of men found themselves unemployed, with no promise or likelihood of a favourable future. Many families survived on soup and the bare necessities. Nobody had new clothes. Life savings were wiped out.

It was the worst of times, unlike any this province had seen before or has seen since. Despair overwhelmed the spirit of the people and the longer the depression lasted the harder it became to cling to any shred of hope. If you were the head of a family and out of work, it was a wretched time.

It was from this abyss of hopelessness that one of the most innovative and timely ideas in Regina's history sprang. The dry weather had taken its toll on Wascana Lake. The lack of rain, the endless waves of heat, the well-muscled Saskatchewan wind, all had licked most of the water from the lake. There were barren spots everywhere. The lake was drying up before the very eyes of the people of Regina and nobody could figure out what to do.

Along came a politician named Jimmy Bryant. He was the minister of public works in the provincial government. He also was a man of innovation and vision.

Jimmy Bryant put together a plan that would pack a one-two punch of good news, one that would produce the kind of results that the people of Regina would still be benefiting from in 2004. Jimmy Bryant saw the drought and the depleting water levels of Wascana Lake as an opportunity to send men into the lake bottom to deepen the lake by about two feet.

Who would do the work? The unemployed men of Regina, that's who. And what would be the long-term benefits? Not only would the lake have more depth, but from the dirt taken from the lake bottom would emerge two islands – Willow and Spruce – that would still be there decades and decades later. And, of course, men without work would find work for a couple of months, hard and exhausting as it would be.

There are very few records available of exactly what happened in the 1931 Dig. And even fewer photographs. In fact, if there are any photographs around from the 1931 work in The Pit, virtually all of them remain forgotten in somebody's attic.

*photo courtesy of City of Regina Archives B-793*
*Digging out the lake bed to form new islands – September 1931*

27

*photo courtesy of City of Regina Archives A-563*
Lakeview and the old Albert Street Bridge – August 14, 1914

There were many reasons the 1931 Dig did not attract a lot of attention. It must be remembered that, in 1931, Wascana Park was pretty well at the southern tip of the city. There was no Hillsdale or Whitmore Park or Albert Park. Lakeview was still in its formative years. So, not a lot of people could get to the lake to watch the work, or they just did not have any interest in it.

The reason for so few photographs? Unlike today, where every family has at least one camera, there were not a lot of cameras around in 1931, and many of them were large and awkward to handle. But not only that, there was another reason. There was a certain sense of embarrassment in being unemployed, and the 2,000-plus men who were hired to dig out the lake likely would not have taken any pleasure in having their pictures taken doing such a task.

But the job did get done, mostly by men with shovels, by horses pulling wagonloads of dirt, by horses hitched to a very rudimentary grader. The 1931 equipment was primitive by the standards of the millions of dollars worth of equipment that was used on The Big Dig of 2004.

There are people still living in Regina who possess distant memories of the 1931 Dig. Two of them are Clarence Taylor and Jack England. Taylor was 85 in 2004, England 82. They were young boys in 1931.

"I was nine years old when it took place," England recalled. His family ran a Regina jewellry store until it closed in 1985. "We lived in a house at 2700 Angus. Dad built it on the northwest corner in 1921. Dad lost the home in 1937. He couldn't meet the mortgage. There weren't a lot of people buying diamond necklaces then. But I do remember them digging out the lake. It was unbelievable what they did with the equipment they had."

*photo courtesy of City of Regina Archives B-791*
Willow and Spruce Islands were built with soil excavated from the lake – September 1931

*photo courtesy of City of Regina Archives RPL-A-173*
The old Broad Street Bridge

"The formation of the islands was Jimmy Bryant's idea. At the time, he was heavily criticized for it. They thought he'd lost his mind. Oh, he caught heck for that," Taylor recalled. "People were sore about that. They called it Bryant's folly."

The 2,000 unemployed men went into the lake in late summer. "They had to wait until the harvest was over," said Taylor, whose family farmed on land just south of the Regina airport. "Mind you, the harvest wasn't much. I remember my dad planted 2,000 bushels of seed and got 200 bushels out of it. I met this fellow who was working on the job. They were so happy just to get work. He said it only took them two months to get it done and get those islands built. He said there were thousands of men working. They'd work from dawn to dusk and only stop for lunch and to feed the horses."

England laughed when he was asked how much interest the people of Regina had in the 1931 Dig. "In 1931, there really wasn't anything south of the lake. Hillsdale wasn't there. The old Broad Street Bridge was there, but they didn't keep it open in the winter. And there wasn't a lot of traffic. There were not many cars around."

Clarence Taylor also chuckles when he talks about the job. "I don't remember folks stopping to watch it. What was there to see? A bunch of men shoveling dirt? You could see that in your backyard."

With time, the drought and the Great Depression came to an end. But what the 2,000 men accomplished in 1931 was a renewal in the ongoing life of Wascana Lake. The two islands – Spruce and Willow – stand as living, lasting monuments to a desperate time in Regina's history. A time and a project that combined to make a priceless contribution to our city.

*photo courtesy of City of Regina Archives A-541*
The new Albert Street Bridge with trolley lines – February 1938

# Chapter 3 "Got the Ball Rolling"

The need to drain Wascana Lake, dig out millions of cubic metres from its bottom, and have it done in time for the spring runoff did not come out of nowhere.

It had for years been a huge concern of the boating clubs which used Wascana Park for training and holding competitions. The buildup of dirt and goose poop, and the abundance of weeds reaching the surface, had put the lake's future viability in a precarious position.

The initial public pressure to get the job done came from Doug Archer, who served the city as its mayor for 12 years. In the winter of 1999, Archer took to the podium in a downtown Regina hotel ballroom. Delivering the annual mayor's address on the state of the union, he focused the public spotlight on his concern and his vision for Wascana Lake. I attended that luncheon and wrote a column on it, which was published in the January 20, 1999 edition of the *Leader-Post*. This is the column from that time when Wascana Lake became a public issue:

> The mayor of the City of Regina chose the grip of winter to warm the souls of the citizens of Regina last week.
>
> Using the annual mayor's address on the state of the union, Doug Archer shared his vision for a huge project that will benefit not only this generation but also future generations of those lucky enough to call Regina their home.
>
> Mayor Doug says he wants to find a way to clean up Wascana Lake, the body of water he called a jewel in Regina's crown. It's about time.
>
> Wascana Lake has long been both the rose and the thorn in this city's garden. Situated smack in the middle of the city, it has for decades and decades provided both Reginans and visitors to the city with a soothing place to wander. There was even a time when people sailed and swam in the lake. It has been a place to walk through, to jog through. In many ways, it has been the envy of virtually every Canadian city.

It's also been a place where the odour it gives up signals the arrival of spring. One of the most trying experiences of life in Regina is to be trapped on the Albert Street Bridge when the lake has thawed and the scent of all those weeds comes free. It is to weep. And gag.

The lake desperately needs some work. That it is man-made is the problem. Over time, the bottom of Wascana Lake has filled in, to the point where weeds are everywhere, swimming is nowhere, sailboating is out, and only the rowers are able to move across it without seriously getting snagged.

Archer's vision will take care of that. His dream is to have the lake dredged in time for the 100th anniversary of Saskatchewan in 2005, in time for the staging of the Canada Summer Games here should Regina be awarded those.

It would be a massive job, so massive that nobody is really sure just how much it will cost – the price tag ranging from $6 million all the way to $60 million.

But it would be money well spent. And there is the bottom-line fact that something is going to have to be done to preserve the lake. Those of us who can remember swimming off the docks of the old Regina Boat House know of the joys of not having to leave the city to swim in a lake.

And it wouldn't be the first time that the city, provincial and federal governments locked hands to fix up Wascana Lake.

In 1931 – 68 years ago – Wascana Lake was deepened, its shoreline improved, and the earth that was excavated was used to make the two islands that are still there.

For the one and only time, Wascana Lake was drained in 1931.

How it was done was amazing. The following is taken from a book that was published in 1953 to celebrate Regina's 50th anniversary of being incorporated as a city:

"To provide all possible labour, the use of heavy equipment was prohibited. Earth was loaded by hand shovel, horse drawn dump wagons hauled it to the island sites. Only people without jobs were employed."

A total of 2,107 people moved about 120,000 cubic yards of earth. The total cost was $102,848.51 of which the City of Regina paid $25,712.12 and the provincial and federal governments paid the rest.

*photo by Pat Pettit*
*Doug Archer,*
*Mayor of Regina 1988 to 2000*

The results were obvious. A photograph taken more than 50 years ago shows a Wascana Lake dotted with sailboats, canoes, rowers, swimmers. There was a footbridge from the north shore to Willow Island, and just east of the Albert Street Bridge on the north side of the lake can be seen a large white building.

It's a picture from another time.

And Doug Archer wants to go back to it, to make it all happen again.

It's a dream worth living.

*photo by Roy Antal*
*Wascana Centre employee Kenneth Bone driving the weed whacker*

# Chapter 4 October 2003 – The Beginning

Doug Archer gave birth to the dream of draining Wascana Lake, but the people of Regina had to be patient before they could live it. It took about five years before Archer's vision was turned into reality, and it took some incredible breaks to make it happen.

There were the complainers. For those who spent their recreational hours rowing or kayaking or canoeing, Wascana Lake had become a nightmare. The slow but sure buildup of alluvium and dirt on the bottom of the lake had severely cut back its depth, and weeds had taken over. It became more and more difficult for the paddlers to get around the lake without snagging their oars or paddles on the weeds that reached for the surface, often lingering just below it.

*photo by Barb Schepers*

*Hughes' family photo*
*Regina Rowing Club 1938 – Canadian Champions*
*left to right – Harry Duckett, Newt Hughes, Dick Priest and Jack Peart*

Once the ice broke in the spring, the state of the lake was clear to both those near it and those on it. Motorists crossing the Albert Street Bridge kept their windows rolled up tightly as the stench from the weeds was often too much. Those on the lake, rowing, were increasingly frustrated by the weeds which hid in the dark water, like an octopus waiting to wrap its tentacles around any intruder – in this case, the oars.

The Regina Rowing Club was the most vocal of any of the organizations which used Wascana Lake to train and hold meets. From first-hand experience the club members could see and feel how quickly Wascana Lake was deteriorating. The Regina Rowing Club had a long and glorious history on the lake, dating back decades to a time when their clubhouse and docks sat on Willow Island and people swam and dove from them. One of the many great moments in the history of the club came in 1938. It was then that the Regina Rowing Club team of Harry Duckett, Newt Hughes, Dick Priest and Jack Peart won the Canadian fours championship. The irony of prairie boys winning a national rowing championship was not lost on the east- and west-coast teams they beat.

With the urging of the various clubs that used Wascana Lake, with the urgency of saving the lake, of preventing it from becoming a marsh, and with the awarding of the 2005 Canada Summer Games to Regina, the door to government funding to deepen Wascana Lake was pried open. But it was veteran Regina MP Ralph Goodale who kicked the door wide open, announcing, in his role as Public Works minister, that the federal government would kick in $9 million to save Wascana Lake from becoming a marsh and to enable other enhancements to the lake to be undertaken. With that money assured, the provincial and City of Regina governments came up with the other $9 million for a total tab of $18 million. The province kicked in $5 million, the city coughed up $4 million. Done deal.

*photo by Designer Photographic Technologies*
*Wascana MP Ralph Goodale*

Goodale, Premier Lorne Calvert and Mayor Pat Fiacco were all smiles on Friday, October 3 when the funding announcement was made. But nobody was smiling more than the Wascana Centre Authority and the people of Regina who use the park and whose numbers would swell once the job was done.

Once the announcement was made, the fun began.

Overseeing the whole project was a Regina company, Clifton Associates, a highly respected engineering firm with a solid international reputation. Wayne Clifton, the president of the company, saw the Wascana Lake project with the eager eyes of a child on Christmas morning. He was excited, to say the least, at being handed the reins. "A project like this basically comes along once in a lifetime," he said. He called the project the pièce de résistance of a 40-year career. He had been involved in the building of Saskatchewan's highway system as well as its northern roads. He had worked on mining and power development in northern Saskatchewan as well as projects throughout North America and around the world. But he had never taken on a task like this.

*photo by Don Healy*
*Mayor Pat Fiacco, Premier Lorne Calvert, Minister Ralph Goodale and Wayne Clifton*

Clifton was among the most highly thought of engineers in Canada. He would, in November of 2003, receive the Lieutenant-Governor's Meritorious Achievement Award for his contributions to the engineering profession. Clifton was accepting tenders for the job within a day of the announcement. Time was definitely a factor. The lake would have to be drained of its existing water and the work would have to be completed by the time the spring thaw and runoff came along in March.

The announcement was the climax to three months of intense preparation. The design had to be finalized; public meetings were held; approvals had to be received from provincial and federal environmental departments.

Within no time at all, two other highly thought of and proven Saskatchewan companies had come on board, and the wheels were swiftly swinging into motion. Broda Construction, based out of Prince Albert, a company started from scratch by Cas Broda of Kamsack, was hired to handle the deepening of the lake. And Dominion Construction of Regina was there to handle the rest. Three Saskatchewan companies – Clifton, Broda and Dominion – brought together to handle one of the biggest jobs in Regina's history.

But before it all began, before they went into the lake and pulled the plug and started draining it, there was a brief interlude. That came on Sunday, October 5, only two days after the announcement, when a lone bull moose wandered into Wascana Lake, shoulder deep in the water near the Saskatchewan Centre of the Arts. The moose soon left, leaving behind photographs and memories of another exciting moment in Wascana Centre.

*photo by Jordan Nicurity*
*Wascana Park has many visitors*

*photos by Roy Antal and Bryan Schlosser*

*As the lake was drained, some strange sights were observed*

On October 15th, the project officially got under way. They began to drain the water out of Wascana Lake. The place would never be the same again. "It's going to take about four or five days to drain off 95 per cent of the lake," was the forecast given by Ken Dockham, director of operations with Wascana Centre Authority. "But you know, the lake isn't that deep to begin with."

The water went fast, leaving behind the aftermath of time as workers uncovered debris that had been thrown into the lake, or left there, over the years. There were old bath tubs, bikes, a chair was found. But nothing really exciting. People were actually expecting that guns would be found and old crimes would be solved. No such high drama. The water left the lake, and it left behind a bunch of junk. Unsolved Crimes would have to wait for another day. There was no smoking gun at the bottom of the lake. Just goose poop and dirt, dreck and debris.

But as the lake was draining, something new was happening. It was a forerunner to what would happen throughout the long hard winter which was approaching. People were flocking to the shores of the mighty Wascana, just to watch, just to take pictures. They realized that history was unfolding before their very eyes. They knew that this was a once-in-a-lifetime opportunity.

Wayne Wilson, a Regina resident for nearly 30 years, took one look and started taking pictures. "I'm curious and fascinated by the fact they're draining the lake and going to improve it," he said. He was going to send the photos to friends who used to live in Regina.

Nearby stood Howard McCall. He had lived in Regina his whole 79 years. He was amazed at how shallow it was. "It used to be deep enough you could swim in it and they had a shack for swimmers."

The draining of the lake was not without its problems. The lake bed was gooey and sticky and it did not take much weight to sink into it. A Wolverine all-track vehicle went onto the lake bed to retrieve some of the junk that had been found and promptly came to a sludgy halt. Another Wolverine was sent into the lake bed to tow it out, but couldn't do it. They did finally get it out, but not without a struggle. The lake bed was not about to surrender its booty easily.

photo by Roy Antal

*Paul Omilion of Tactical Amphibious Ground Support stuck in the mud*

*photo by Roy Antal*

*Wascana Centre employees Martin Beler (left) and Lynette Smith*

By the end of the month, the winter weather was threatening to take hold. The first snow came on October 29th, sheathing the city in a white cover. As the temperatures began to drop, concern rose in the Wascana Centre Authority building, which sits on the east shore of the lake near the marina. The Authority workers were on the lake bed with pumps, drawing out the remaining pools of water. The additional moisture would only end up draining into the lake and, if the temperatures dropped too much, it would cause problems for the pumps.

As October passed to November, the level of anticipation increased. The last of the water had yet to be drained, but there were no major concerns as soon it would freeze and winter would be at hand, ready to offer the workers one challenge after another as The Big Dig continued through its early stages.

# Chapter 5 November & December 2003

It was a November to remember, one unlike any Regina had seen in years, if ever.

The city sprang alive in mid-November when it was thrust upon the national stage by the hosting of the Grey Cup festival and game. Hotels were booked. Party venues were wall-to-wall people. The streets were packed with out-of-towners enjoying Regina's hospitality. The city wore a big smile. On the Sunday of the game between the Montreal Alouettes and the Edmonton Eskimos, Taylor Field was packed with fans from one end of the country to the other, even from as far away as Baltimore.

But there was another activity taking place that also generated tons of enthusiastic interest. Like a magnet, Wascana Lake continued to draw people to its shores, despite the cool breath of winter.

By the middle of November, most of the water had been drained from Wascana Lake, and much of what was left had frozen. There was an erie feeling to the place when you drove by, a vast emptiness, only a few confused geese on the lake bed. And, always, people with cameras.

The interest now was in the continuing process to prepare the lake for the heavy equipment that would be coming in, and also to ensure there were efficient ways for the dirt to be hauled out of the lake. While, initially, it may have been thought that the lake bed would freeze and thus be able to support the rock trucks carrying the dirt, the people in charge of the project were now looking at an easier way.

*photo by Bryan Schlosser*
*Technicians working for Clifton Associates*

They decided the best way would be to build dirt roads from the lake to the places where the dirt would be dumped, as nearby as the hill in Douglas Park and as far away as the east side of the Ring Road, near SIAST and Riverside Cemetery. The roads would have to be built under the Broad Street Bridge and the Ring Road bridge. That's what was eventually done, and it proved to be an efficient way to move the dirt. Had they used city streets to get it to its destinations, the streets would have been torn apart and traffic would have been disrupted.

*photo by Jordan Nicurity*
*Wascana watchers*

Wayne Clifton, the man running the show, knew there was plenty of work to be done, in a relatively short period of time, before the actual excavation took place.

"The whole lake has to be fenced," said Clifton, and soon the orange mesh fence went up, and the signs warning people to stay away were hammered in place. "Then, they start working on the two bridges, to build haul roads underneath them to allow the earth movers and the trucks to move underneath them.

"And they'll be mobilizing equipment and building their shops and setting up administrative offices. So they will move very quickly, setting up the logistics to support the operation."

Not only that, but November marked the time when the surveying work of the lake bed would take place, to determine just how much dirt would have to be taken out of it to achieve the desired depth of between 4 and 5.5 metres.

The excitement reached a new level when Dominion Construction was awarded the general contract for the revitalization and deepening of Wascana Lake. Dominion wasted no time in marshalling its equipment

photo by Don Healy
*Makeshift dirt roads were built*

north of SIAST on the east side of the Ring Road, next door to the entrance to the Wascana Golf and Country Club. By mid-November, the weather had warmed. It was a mixed blessing. "It will help construction crews who have to erect 2,700 metres of security fence along the lake's shoreline, but at the same time it means we can't start digging," said Dominion senior vice-president Brian Barber.

Trailers were being set up at various sites in the park. The white trailers were pulled into a spot near SIAST, where Broda would be headquartered. The rock-truck drivers would come here for their schedules, receive their pay, and board buses that would take them out onto the lake bed to the equipment they would operate. It would be a staging area for the incredible action that was yet to come.

Over by the old Broad Street Bridge, more white trailers were put up. This is where you would find the people from Dominion Construction, trooping in and out of the trailers wearing in hard hats. Nearby was the security trailer. The fences were now in place, ringing Wascana Lake like an orange ribbon, and it was up the security people to make sure nobody went down on the lake bottom that shouldn't be there.

photo by Roy Antal
*Dominion's trailers near Broad Street Bridge*

Clifton himself was getting more and more excited. He was suddenly a popular figure in Regina. He was being invited to speak to various groups and organizations in town. Clearly, The Big Dig was the talk of Regina.

A little over a week before the end of November, Clifton found himself at a podium speaking to a luncheon meeting sponsored by the Saskatchewan Environmental Industry and Managers Association and Saskatchewan Environment.

photo by Roy Antal
*Wayne Clifton, President of Clifton Associates*

The environment was a major concern when work began on the lake. And Clifton was very careful to make sure regulations were followed to the final period. An environmental issue forced cancellation of one project. Goose Island was to have been expanded, but somebody raised a concern about it. The government agency overseeing The Big Dig, Saskatchewan Property Management Corporation, listened and decided to leave Goose Island alone.

"We are at the end of the assessment period and all of the permits are in place," Clifton told the luncheon crowd. "Digging this kind of a hole with this kind of equipment, 500 metres from the Hotel Saskatchewan, is really quite a challenge. The contractor has to be careful because public safety is a great concern, and so is environmental safety."

Clifton's enthusiasm for the job continued to spill over. By the time the project was done, Clifton said, "People can expect to see game fish and a beach (at the marina) to be added as well. I hope to see people fishing off the sidewalk in the near future." His grin told it all.

By the end of November, the job was taking on a new look. Broda was beginning to move in some of its equipment, hauling it into Regina on the backs of long semi-trailer trucks. They would be coming to Regina with their great yellow cargo from other areas in Saskatchewan, Canada, the United States and Belgium. Yes, Belgium. A huge hoe with a giant bucket was built in Belgium for the job, taken by ship to the United States, and brought to Regina on a semi-trailer. The $1-million baby would be something to see. It could fill a truck in a matter of mere moments.

*photo by Bryan Schlosser*
*The giant Caterpillar mass excavator arrives*

By early December, some of the Broda crew were in The Pit, draining off the remaining water. The park was now in the grip of winter. The ground was white, the flowers had long gone, and the trees, empty of leaves, were little more than grey skeletons standing as sentinels on the shoreline.

Safety issues continued to be a huge concern for Dominion Construction. Project manager Mark Behrns said that Dominion had double-fenced the entire perimeter of the lake and assigned full-time security people to patrol the surrounding areas during construction, which, at full head, would be going on 24 hours a day, seven days a week.

Work crews also were hard at work grooming the bottom of the lake for the equipment that soon would venture onto it.

By the of December, much of the preparation work had been completed and the lake now awaited the arrival of the machinery that would make the miracle happen, in an often wild chase to beat the deadline.

## CHAPTER 6 JANUARY 2004

**T**hey were huge. And long. And they looked so powerful. They came from all directions, rolling convoys of armour carrying the machinery of a miracle. The big semi-trailers rumbled into the city without much fanfare. Rusty Clunie, with Broda Construction, and Mark Behrns, the project manager from Dominion Construction, were two of the happiest people in town to see them coming. And Wayne Clifton could now see the toys that would help realize the crowning moment of his great career.

*Construction continues on Wascana Lake on a frosty winter day*

photo by Bryan Schlosser

On the flatbeds could be seen the great yellow equipment that would be used to clear away the bottom of Wascana Lake, to increase its depth to an average of 5.5 metres and bring back the majesty of the centerpiece of Wascana Centre. They had assembled the most impressive amount of heavy equipment this city had ever seen, and they had their work cut out for them. There were large hoes and rock trucks, big Cats, small hoes, and men who knew how to operate them at the highest level of efficiency. They were men's men, as resilient as steel. They knew their stuff. They wore the uniforms of men who work outdoors. The blue jeans, faded, torn, but comfortable; the thick shirts lined in fleece. Their faces showed the dark shadows of four days of freedom from razor blades. They slumped back in metal chairs when not out in The Pit, their hard hats pushed back on their heads, the coffee in their hands hot and refreshing. The faces were lined by the ridges of time. Their eyes always seemed tired when they rested, but came bright and alive when they were taken down to their machinery.

The lake had been still, void of activity over the Christmas holidays. Everybody went home to be with their families, to indulge in a final rest before coming back to Regina in the New Year when they would be spending the better part of the next three months sitting in the cabs of the machinery, or sleeping. This would be no place for the faint of heart.

The lake itself had taken on the strangest appearance during the lull of the holiday season. I can remember one early morning in January when the weather was frigid and the sun was just coming up over the white eastern horizon. The wind was still. Nothing was moving. From the moment The Big Dig had started, and the first of the equipment had been moved in, I made it a habit to drive through the park on the way to work and on the way home. Sometimes, I would be sitting at my desk and nothing would be happening on my keyboard, so I would put on my coat and drive through the park. I might as well have moved into the place, I was spending so much time there.

*photo by Bryan Schlosser*
*The cold weather could not stop Broda's men*

On this morning, all was quiet. I did not even have the radio on. The park was empty of sound and lights and people. I could hear the snow crunching under my tires. As I drove north along the parkway, I stopped near the fountain that sits east of the Legislative Building. I looked out over the lake, to Willow Island, to the north side, to the south side, to the east side. The water had long been drained out of the lake and now it was a picture of patches of snow and dirt set in the shadows of the rising sun. It was so empty of life. Soon, everything would be changed. Forever. The lake bed would first be stripped of the top three feet of dirt, and then the serious digging would take place. The plan called for the digging to begin east of the Broad Street Bridge, move north to the end of the lake and then turn west to the Albert Street Bridge. Along the way, a new island, Pine Island, would be created by amputating the land at the old Broad Street Bridge abutment, turning it into an island that would feature a waterfall.

The floor of the lake would be filled with the big yellow machinery, the rock trucks coming and going in a steady stream, the constant groaning of equipment that would never be shut down unless something had gone wrong. The shores would soon be lined with an ever-flowing river of people, so curious, armed with their cameras, plugging into history.

Wascana Lake would never be the same.

The headline in the *Leader-Post* of January 8th, a Thursday, read: "It fills a truck in three scoops."

*photo by Don Healy*
*Broda crews going under the Broad Street Bridge*

The story was about the early January arrival of the biggest hunk of equipment that would settle into Wascana Lake and reach into the its depths. It was a Caterpillar mass excavator – one of the biggest pieces of machinery in the world. It weighed more than 90,000 kilograms. It had a six-cubic-metre bucket and was capable of filling a truck in just three scoops.

*photo by Bob Newton*

*The big Cat's first day on the job.*

When Broda Construction was awarded the job of digging out the lake, Gord Broda, son of owner Cas, and Rusty Clunie, general manager, went to work at sizing up the equipment they would need to get the job done in time. They had their eye on the big Cat and went through Kramer Ltd. in Regina to get it. The rest is history, of the most bizarre kind.

Caterpillar has plants all over the world. The one used to build the piece of equipment destined for Regina was in Belgium. When the call came from Kramer to buy one, at about $1 million, it was put on a ship, which sailed across the Atlantic Ocean, in the grey damp cold of winter, to Baltimore. It was moved onto a semi-trailer and on to Regina it went.

The giant track hoe would become the mechanical celebrity of The Big Dig.

The action started just east of the Broad Street Bridge.

The dirt roads had been built, rising several feet above the lake bed, and the rock trucks were rumbling atop them, carrying their cargo to the four chosen sites. The roads ran all the way from the dump sites on the east side of the Ring Road, under the Ring Road bridge,

*photo by Bryan Schlosser*

*A crew from Kramer Ltd. services the Caterpillar mass excavator*

past Douglas Park, the Science Centre, under the Broad Street Bridge and all the way to Albert Street. Mobile strands of bright lights, running off generators, had been set up throughout the bottom of the lake, moving as the workers moved, to ensure the job could continue at night. It made for a surreal scene.

Perhaps, the most revealing moments came when you saw the progress made 12 hours after you had last been there. It was remarkable. They were moving at a rapid clip. Suddenly, almost overnight, no, it was overnight, the new look of Wascana Lake was taking shape.

And before January was two weeks old, people shook off the cold of the winter to come to the lakeside and watch. They came wearing cameras and binoculars, jostling for position on the Broad Street Bridge where the action was. All day long, they were there.

Bob Starkey, who had left Regina to live in Estevan, was among the Wascana Lake groupies. "I used to walk around this lake almost every day for five years prior to moving away," he said. "When I was a young boy living in this city, I actually swam in this lake, so it's nice to see them doing it because I think it's a real asset for the City of Regina and it's a real showpiece. It's an excellent project. I think it's really one of the main features of the City of Regina and I think people are proud of it and like to see this happen." Starkey even admitted to the thought that if he could, he might some day again swim in Wascana Lake. "If they got it deep enough and if they put a facility in I'd do it just for old time's sake."

photo by Josh Sawka

*The Big Dig became a place of lasting memories*

The flow of people around the lake continued unabated.

"I think it's really one of the main features of the City of Regina," is how Regina resident Kay Finch described it between taking photos on a Sunday afternoon in January. "I think people are proud of it and like to see this happen. I was here when we used to be able to go swimming in Wascana so it's a pretty historic event as far as I'm concerned."

Alfred Aichinger, who has lived in Regina since 1959, described The Big Dig as an "event. You don't build a lake every day. Maybe once in a lifetime."

There was the odd casualty as the work continued in sometimes freezing weather. It was announced in mid-January that Waskimo, the city's annual winter festival, would not be held in 2004. It has always been held on Wascana Lake and there was no substitute for it in the city.

By the end of January, the mood of the city was upbeat, strange in the face of the harsh winter that was at hand, strange because this normally is a time of year when the best that is yet to come, which would be spring, seemed so far away. But the digging at Wascana Lake was the most positive thing to happen to

Regina in quite some time, and people were plugging into it at every turn. They could see the progress every day and watching it happen gave everybody a lift.

By the end of January, the men and machinery had moved tons of dirt from the lake bottom, and were at the turn in the lake and heading west to the Albert Street Bridge. Pine Island had been built. Spruce Island had been enlarged. The 8 metre (26-foot) deep fish hole just east of Spruce Island had been dug out. Not only that, but work was under way in building the foundations for the piers at the new promenade deck.

The march against time was right on schedule.

photo by Roy Antal

*The old Broad Street Bridge abutment area becomes a new island with a waterfall – to the left of Pine Island is the fish sanctuary*

# Chapter 7  In The Pit

From the very moment The Big Dig began and the lake started to take on its new shape, I was, I admit, mesmerized by it all. I have always felt that this lake was something special in my life, from the day in the late 1940s my mother and father took me to the Regina Rowing Club boat house on Willow Island. I would swim off the dock, run around and play, get picked up and thrown into the water by friends of my parents.

When I began to work at the *Leader-Post*, in 1962, I lived in a boarding house at 2341 McIntyre Street. I often walked over to Wascana Park and strolled through it. When I became a parent to two boys, our Saturday and Sunday mornings were reserved for walks through the park. They would last for hours. In summer, we would be washed by the warm morning sun and fanned by a cool breeze coming off the water. In the beginning, I would push their strollers along the paths, from one side of the lake to the other, and when they grew older we would play soccer, or hide and seek, or ride our bikes. On other days, I would wake up early in the mornings, around 5 or so, and I would start my day with a ride through the park. I would go all around the lake, stopping at Robin's Donuts across the street from the Golden Mile Shopping Centre to pick up gossip and ending up at my aunt and uncle's, Gordon and Irene Heenan, around 6:30 for breakfast, or at least a coffee.

*Saskatchewan History and Folklore Society – Everett Baker Collection*

*The boat club was always a busy place*

Wascana Centre was the promising child of vision and imagination. It was, I am sure, the result of a realization by one of the early settlers of Regina that the place they had ultimately chosen to become the capital city of Saskatchewan was somewhat barren. It was in the middle of nowhere – latitude 50.26N, longitude 104.40W, altitude 577m. Nowhere. It was surrounded by prairie, as empty of trees as the Sahara Desert, as flat as a pancake. When the wind blew, it would raise dust from the dry soil and send it whirling across the flatness. It was a place of infinite distances, where the early settlers could see forever, or at least until the empty fields met up with the blue Saskatchewan sky sprawling across the horizon and disappearing into a burnt orange sunset that could lift the soul. Somebody, sometime, back then, decided there was a need for trees to be planted, a park to be built, a lake to be developed. And, so, as is the way of the people here, they did it themselves. They did. And our generation has benefited from this moment of inspiration, this creation of the greatest masterpiece of man-made nature in the nation.

I knew all of this. I felt all of this. The place has always been so special to me, as it has been to so many others who lived in the city, or visited it. We are truly the benefactors of this gift from the city's forefathers.

Somebody once said to me, and I have never forgotten it, "We take Wascana Park for granted. We don't realize how lucky we are to have it. We may get droughts. We may get blizzards. We may even get the odd tornado. We always get mosquitos. But we also have a place within an easy drive from home where we can rest and relax and enjoy ourselves in our very own park."

All of that came back to me in January of 2004 as I drove through the park, tracking the unstoppable march of man and machine as they forged a deeper lake and a better park.

And I can remember, so many times, thinking, no, wishing, that I would give anything to, just once, be able to go down into The Pit and see what it looked like from there, to hear the machinery, feel the machinery, smell the burnt diesel fuel, look up and see the shoreline. It would be such a journey.

One morning in January, the phone rang in my office. I picked it up. It was Mark Behrns, the project manager from Dominion Construction, a guy I had known for a number of years, mostly through his tireless devotion to the Saskatchewan Roughriders. I was always assured of seeing him every year at the Riders' fundraising Plaza of Honor Dinner.

"You want to go down in The Pit?" he said.

"God, yes," I answered.

We set up a time.

*photo by Don Mathieson*

*A view of Wascana Bandshell from The Pit*

The next day, the phone rang again. This time, it was Cas Broda, the founder of Broda Construction, calling from Kamsack, where the company began.

"I have been reading your columns on Wascana Lake," he said, "and I am wondering if you would like to go down in one of the trucks and see what it is like for yourself. All you have to do is phone my son, Gordie, and tell him you want to go down there and he will take care of it. Any time, you call him."

*A massive job still lies ahead*

*photo by Roy Antal*

The view from the shore of the lake was of a valley being formed by the machinery that was gouging dirt from the ground and dumping it into rock trucks, which took their payload on a winding journey under bridges and over makeshift dirt roads to the other side of the highway. The view from the bottom was something I could only imagine. Until Mark Behrns and Cas Broda phoned me.

So, I went down into The Pit with Mark Behrns and Rusty Clunie, who was Broda's main man on the scene. I felt much, saw lots, and will never forget it. It was a miserably cold day, the wind blowing hard, biting into you with sharp blades – sheer, frigid and penetrating. I didn't care. I was going into The Pit. This is the column I wrote about my trip into The Pit for the first time. It appeared in the *Leader-Post* on Friday, January 30, 2004:

### The Pit is a thing of wonder

The PIT – The place has no quiet. Not for a moment. Even when the temperature is at a record low.

"The equipment never stops," says Rusty Clunie.

"We can't stop, we just keep going," laughs Mark Behrns.

The equipment keeps rumbling, no matter what is happening. We are in a truck in the afternoon of a frigid day this week, moving down into the ever expanding pit that is the bottom of Wascana Lake, and now has become the gathering place for the greatest massing of giant machinery this city has ever seen. Nowhere in this country has something like this ever been attempted: first the draining of a lake and now the ongoing marvel that is the deepening of the lake.

Behrns is the project manager, an employee of Dominion Construction. Clunie is the general manager of Broda Construction out of Kamsack, the company that owns all the equipment and has done huge jobs all over the country. "It's the first time we've done something like this in an urban setting," says Clunie. These are the two most important people involved in this project. They are responsible for everything day to day, minute to minute. They are remarkable people in charge of so much. But, clearly, they are enjoying this – the magnitude of it, the steady march across the lake bottom, each second that clicks off the clock adding to the pressure of getting the lake deepened before spring runoff.

*photo by Roy Antal*

*Rusty Clunie, Gord Broda, Brian Barber, Mark Behrns*

This is how big the job is. It will cost around $18 million. There are 22 rock trucks with huge tires as tall as men. Thirteen of the trucks are the big ones. There are nine track hoes to scoop up the dirt, to move, to dig. One of the hoes was made in Belgium and shipped to North America where it was trucked to Regina, where it is used 24 hours a day. It has a huge bucket and can fill a truck in two scoops. It costs about $1 million, but it pays its way. There are 92 people here working for Broda, driving the trucks, operating the hoes, doing whatever has to be done. They work in 12-hour shifts. The shift changes are so smooth, they rarely lose more than 10 minutes from the job. They will spend about $1 million on fuel by the time this is over. There are 25 people working here on the concrete end of it for Dominion Construction.

*Construction crews taking advantage of the weather*
*photos by Roy Antal*

*photo by Bryan Schlosser*

Clunie is driving the truck as we go onto the lake bed on the coldest of days. "We'll go over to the fill site, where it all started, and that'll make it easier to see how all of this is happening."

We get there on a road Broda Construction built when they arrived here, wide enough and solid enough to handle the never-ending traffic of these rock trucks as they go back and forth, hundreds of times a day. The roads lead to three sites where the dirt is dumped, all on the east side of the Trans-Canada Highway. The roads are remarkably smoother than many of Regina's paved streets.

*Coming and going under the Broad Street Bridge*

We turn around, near the Wascana Golf Club, and head down the wide packed dirt road, the rock trucks moving past us in the other direction. It takes each rock truck approximately 15 minutes to make the round trip, once the truck is loaded. The trucks can go as fast as 45 kilometres per hour. "When everything is right, they're really rocking and rolling," says Rusty.

We pass under the highway at the Assiniboia turn-off, and roll past Douglas Park, where the hill will be turned into a bigger recreation site.

Now we are going past the wooden structure that crosses the east side of the lake at the Saskatchewan Science Centre. "We'll be taking that out of here," says Mark.

*The old wooden bridge by the Science Centre is being taken down*

*photo by Don Healy*

*A quiet moment under the bridge*

We go under the Broad Street Bridge, and now, right before us, as the truck climbs from the slope from under the bridge, is a scene that leaves you in awe, which brings almost into your face exactly what is being done here in our city by companies and people from our province who excel at their jobs.

This is Ground Zero of this project. By the time they have finished, sometime in mid-March they hope, they will have moved over 1.5 million cubic metres of soil.

Straight ahead of us is the concrete wall of the old Broad Street Bridge. It will be turned into a waterfall. And it will be an island, the south side of it having been cut away, and it will be called Pine Island. Out on the lake, Spruce and Willow Islands, built from the dirt removed in large part by men with shovels in the 1930s, will be enlarged.

Exactly east of Spruce Island, the activity is fierce. The Belgium-made track hoe is filling one rock truck after another, a steady stream of yellow monsters coming and going. It is here, a few feet east of Spruce Island, that the lake will be the deepest. While the rest of the lake between the Albert and Broad Street bridges will be deepened to a depth of about 5.5 metres, or about 18 feet, this long narrow spot just off the east shores of Spruce Island will be made even deeper. "It'll be the fish pond," says Mark. It will be the winter refuge for fish.

*photo by Adrien Bolen*

*Earthmoving machines in action*

*Scoop by scoop, the lake is deepened and shaped*

photo by Bryan Schlosser

I ask how they, as they are working, know just how deep they have dug and how they maintain level ground. "We've got lasers on the equipment," says Rusty, "and we've got guys out there checking all the time."

Moving down the lake, you can see where the walls of the lake will be strengthened and walkways and viewing points added. You can see where the fountain, about 7.5 metres (25 feet) tall, will be placed. As you move to the far end of the lake, to the Albert Street Bridge, there is again action. More rock trucks and a track hoe are on the go. It is here, in the shadow of the bridge, that the promenade is being built that will carry cyclists, walkers and joggers across the lake. The pedestrian bridge will be about 6 metres (20 feet) wide.

photo by Cheryl Pady

*The promenade by the Albert Street Bridge takes shape*

The magnitude of all of this is impossible to get hold of. And the men in charge are spending no time unwisely, or without massive planning and concise schedules. "We were on site, I would say, 7 to 10 days after we got the job," says Clunie. The Broda equipment came here from all over Canada and, of course, Belgium. "It took 13 semi-trailers to get it all here," he says.

Out on the lake bed, 24 hours a day, through blizzards and everything else, the track hoes dig and the rock trucks rumble. The noise is music to the ears of anybody who cares about the lake, or the city. No city in this country has ever tried something this big before. Only in Regina, you say. Of course.

photo by Bob Newton

*Earth pile growing near SIAST – University of Regina in the background*

photo by Gerald Lindenbach

*Intense action in The Pit*

*A balancing act*

photo courtesy of
Saskatchewan Property Management Corporation

*Night dig*

photo by Jordan Nicurity

# CHAPTER 8 FEBRUARY 2004

The winter has not been kind to anybody working outside. Intense cold has arrived, the kind that goes right through you. A series of blizzards, raging prairie snow storms, came from nowhere and stayed too long. There were times when the city seemed paralyzed. Great snow drifts shut down the Ring Road, the Lewvan, and made traveling inside Regina treacherous. In some places there was no movement. Even the city's street cleaning crews couldn't get out. Danger also beckoned outside the city. Multi-car pileups involving semi-trailer trucks tied up the Trans-Canada Highway east of the city. Airplanes couldn't land, or take off.

*photo by Don Healy*

*A large mining rock truck*

Twice, within a two week period, even The Big Dig was forced to head for cover. But it was the last to go. Two vicious blizzards – one on the second last day of January and the other one 10 days into February – brought the work in Wascana Lake to a halt. The crews from Broda and Dominion had worked through much of the two storms, and would have kept going had they been able to see.

But when visibility became totally obscured by the blinding, swirling snow, driven by mighty winds, the danger level for the drivers and their equipment became too high. It was like being in the middle of a blender. So, they shut down, knowing time lost on the Big Dig at this stage of the year could become a serious issue in getting the job done in time. The planners of the job could build no reliable backup plans in the timeline. Who could predict when spring would arrive and when the runoff would begin? You could only hold it back for a limited amount of time. Once it started, the lake would fill with water, whether the job was done or not.

*Storm brewing – just before the second whiteout*

photos by Bob Newton

*photo by Jason Gasmo*
*One after another, the rock trucks were on the move*

The cold was never really the issue with the people from Broda who ran the equipment in The Pit. The cold, they could handle. It was only when visibility became an issue and put them in a position of peril that work was stopped. The cold drew out their courage and their devotion to the job they were doing. Men working on machinery, outside, on the lake bottom, in cold, cold weather, wearing no gloves. That is what they were all about.

By February 11th, about 45 per cent of the lake bed had been dug out, leaving 55 per cent to complete in just over a month, to be sure the job would get done. Ken Dockham, director of operations for Wascana Centre Authority, had a view of the lake and the weather from his office on the east side the Wascana Centre. He had a worried look when the weather shut the operation down in February. "It will have a big impact when we have such a narrow window to get the work done. We need to get back in operation as soon as we can and hope that production rates can improve," he said.

The pressure to get the job done by the year 2004 was intense because of the Canada Summer Games that would be coming in 2005.

"If the Games weren't being held in 2005, there would not be the same need to get it done this year," Dockham said. Some of the major water sports, of course, would be using Wascana Lake. Nobody wanted to present the visitors to the city with an unfinished product. They wanted it postcard perfect.

*photo by Roy Antal*
*Ken Dockham in The Big Dig display room at the Wascana Centre building*

*photo by Roy Antal*

*Work near the Broad Street Bridge and the roadway in front of the Centre of the Arts*

So, the pace of the work quickened. The ideal temperature for the job was -15°C. That would keep the makeshift roads frozen and firm and it would not be so cold as to interfere with the equipment, which stopped running only when repairs were needed. Gas tanker trucks came into The Pit to refuel the equipment as it worked, and by the time the job was over it would have consumed over $2 million worth of diesel fuel.

The digging had started January 5th, a Monday, and had kept going virtually 24 hours a day, seven days a week. On Valentine's Day they had been at it for 40 days and Regina's love affair with the project continued. People continued to stream through the park to watch the work being done. "We're surprised there aren't any accidents on Ring Road or Broad Street," Dominion project manager Mark Behrns said. Cars regularly slowed or came to a full stop on both roads when they were passing the sites. Even when the weather turned terribly cold, they continued to come.

Forty days into the job, it was taking a defined shape. They had virtually finished digging out the fish hole just east of Spruce Island to a depth of 8 metres. You could stand on the south side of the lake and see the deepening of the race lane running straight up the lake. You could see the newly created Pine Island where a waterfall will be built, using the cement wall from the old Broad Street Bridge as its backing, with a pathway so you can walk along the island and under the waterfall. The best way to explain what would be different would be to say that previously the lake had been a pool of water on a plate, when the job was done the plate would be replaced by a bowl.

*They hauled out 1.4 million cubic metres*

photo by Roy Antal

The whole project was so well planned, there were few surprises. But one surprise was the amount of dirt that would have to be taken from the bottom of the lake. They had originally estimated 1.2-million cubic metres would be hauled out, but once they got into the job the figure climbed to more than 1.4-million, which added about another five days of work if they were to maintain a pace of taking out 25,000 cubic metres a day. There was much more goose poop and weed decay than was first thought and, in the beginning of the job, it acted as an insulator, keeping the ground under it from freezing. But they had cleaned it out, and now it was February, and Ken Dockham was optimistic that all would end well.

'If spring holds off, we'll be okay," said Dockham.

*Working in a winter wonderland*

photo by Norma Jean Cook

Rusty Clunie, Broda's general manager, continued to push the project along. Broda, the company that had started 47 years earlier in Kamsack, with one gravel truck, now had 22 rock trucks, nine excavators/track hoes, eight crawler dozers, three loaders, four motor scrapers, two graders and four compactors working in the lake site, and about 100 workers.

Clunie recognized the importance of the job. "The state of the lake from the point it was originally dug had reached a point of almost non-use," he said. "You were going to end up with a slough in the middle of Regina so something had to be done."

The workers, more used to building roads in the north and working in mines, had never taken on a project like this before. And the guys driving the trucks and working the rest of the equipment began to take on a celebrity status in the city, to the crowds that were drawn to them on a daily basis. People, it seemed, couldn't get enough of watching The Big Dig and they marveled at the efficiency of these men under the hard hats, labouring in the cabs of their equipment.

Late in February, an old photograph was found by an amateur photographer named Grant McDonald. It was taken in the 1920s and it was of a sign stuck in the ground of the north side of the lake, with the lake itself and the Legislative Building in the background. The sign read, DANGER, DEEP WATER. McDonald figures the photo was taken in the mid- to late-1920s by his wife's great uncle, Briggs Caverly, which would mean the picture was taken just before the lake was emptied of water and deepened in 1931 by the over 2,000 unemployed men who had been caught by the Great Depression.

*photo courtesy of Grant McDonald*
*In the 1920s, Wascana Lake carried a deep water warning on the north shore*

With a week to go in the month of February, Regina was hit by a wave of warm weather. It was spring-like, with the temperature nearing zero. The weather turned the bottom of the lake, where The Big Dig was ongoing, slick and, at times, muddy, making it difficult for the rock trucks to carry their cargo on the packed dirt roads. For most of the afternoons of the warm spell, productivity slowed by about 25 per cent, but once the sun left and the weather

*photo by Jason Gasmo*

*Warm weather turned the roads into slippery mud*

turned cooler, around seven o'clock every night, the ground would harden and the pace would pick up. To make sure the job would get done, Broda brought in five more trucks and some more loading equipment. The clanging and reverberation of machinery in Wascana Lake intensified.

*photo by Jordan Nicurity*

*Working around the clock, seven days a week*

The other downturn to the warm weather was a rapid increase in the number of people coming to Wascana Park to watch the action. It created some serious traffic issues, with some motorists parking their cars in driving lanes. It resulted in the Wascana Centre Authority handing out a lot of $50 parking tickets.

When February passed and March arrived, over 75 per cent of the excavation had been completed and the end was in sight. As well, piles were being installed on the promenade deck, the precast wall for the promenade bridge was being erected and a retaining wall was being built around Pine Island.

photo by Cerise Zaren

*In the sun of a comfortable day, the work continued*

*photo courtesy of Saskatchewan Property Management Corporation*

Building a retaining wall near the Broad Street Bridge

# Chapter 9 March 2004

The beat picked up. Like Victor Sawa exhorting the Regina Symphony Orchestra to the closing, dramatic moments of a powerful musical selection, Gord Broda and Rusty Clunie were pushing their people into the final moments of The Big Dig. A week into March, everything was moving at a swift pace. And if there can be drama in digging a hole in the ground, then there was high drama blanketing everything in The Pit. The project was well over 75 per cent completed. They would get it done in time for spring runoff!

*photo by Roy Antal*

*The view from above shows the size of the project*

"The main dig from Broad Street to Albert Street is now done," Dominion Construction vice-president Brian Barber said. "Now we are coming back on both the sides to get that dug out, and shaped, and trimmed up, and finish the retaining wall, and get the bridge in there. We are in the downhill stretch."

Broda was hauling about 21,000 cubic metres of dirt out of the lake every day, which put them on a schedule of completion by the third week of March, dangerously close to spring runoff.

People in the thousands were now coming to the lakeside every day to watch the finishing touches being applied to the biggest project this city had ever seen.

One early March day, they were greeted by a strange sight. There was a seven-metre high teepee erected on the north shore of the lake, almost directly across from the Legislative Building. There would be a special First Nations water ceremony. Elders representing the Saulteaux, Dakota, Cree and Assiniboine First Nations, the four main tribes within the southern Saskatchewan Treaty Four area, performed the blessing of the waters of Wascana Lake. The ceremony was closed to the public.

*photo by Cheryl Pady*

*With spring approaching, the pace quickened*

photo by Elise Botero

*Blessing of the water ceremony was held*

The blessing held special meaning for the 29 people, including politicians, who were invited to attend, among them federal finance minister Ralph Goodale, those involved in the actual project, and young First Nations people. One of them was a 17-year-old student, Adam McMurtry, who felt it was important to be involved in such an event. "Having ceremonies like that are good because they get the youth involved so we can pass the information on to the next generation," he said.

The warm March weather continued to slow down the digging a bit, but it also sped up some of the work on the enhancements, a trade-off those running the show were quite happy to accept. It simply meant all that had to be done, before the waters from the winter's melting snow came, would be done.

photo by Brian Cobbledick

*View from under the Trafalger Outlook footbridge on the east side of the lake*

*photo by Bryan Schlosser*

*Leader-Post reporter Barb Pacholik checks out the machinery*

Over the course of the winter, there was a concern among some people that there would not be enough water to fill the deepened lake. But there was enough snow out there, predicted one water expert, to fill 10 Wascana Lakes.

The great gouge in the ground was an amazing sight from the shore. But from down in The Pit it was even more amazing. You never could fully appreciate the size of the equipment, the track hoes and excavators, the rock trucks, until you went down there and stood next to them. The tires of the rock trucks alone were the height of an average man.

The level of interest in The Big Dig was intensifying. A poll conducted by the *Leader-Post* showed that 77 per cent of Regina residents had made an effort to watch the progress of the project. Visitors from other cities were taken down to the lake to watch and to have their pictures taken.

*photo by Andy Buchamer*

*The job over, men and machinery assemble for photographs*

*It all became a blur at night*

photo by Ken Jones

By the middle of March, the project was virtually finished. All that remained to be done was finishing off the enlarging of Willow Island, working on the shoreline in front of the Legislative Building and digging out the marina area.

They continued to work through the night, the generator-operated banks of moving stands of lights looking from a distance as if they were from another planet. The dome of the Legislative Building was lit up as well, a sentinel of sorts, standing watch over the men and their work.

On Saturday, March 20, 2004, the last scoop of dirt came off the 38-hectare lake and was trucked out.

"It's officially, totally completed," said Broda general manager Rusty Clunie. "I'm feeling pretty good. But I'm glad it's over. I've had many a sleepless night waiting to get out of the lake before the water runs. The biggest obstacle was the weather, either the storms or the warm temperatures."

*Broda team lines up*
photo by Bryan Schlosser

*Parked*
photo by Don Healy

*The Crew*
photo by Bryan Schlosser

photo by Roy Antal

*Barbecue for the crew*

On Monday, March 22, in a sight that will likely not be seen in Regina ever again, Broda Construction lined up all of its equipment along the south end of the lake in front of the Legislative Building for a "team" photograph. Later on, Larry Bird, a former Saskatchewan Roughrider and now owner of a number of Regina hotels, felt something should be done for the work crews. So, he brought a big barbecue down to the lake bottom and served up a hot lunch.

photo by Roy Antal

*March 22, 2004, the job over, the equipment leaves the lake bottom in a parade of triumph*

Soon, the lake would be cleared of all the equipment, which would be loaded onto semi-trailer trucks and sent on the next jobs. The men would go to their homes and take a break before Rusty Clunie called them again. The lake bed would be empty, until the spring runoff came in.

By the weekend of March 27/28, the waters had arrived. They came through the temporary dam at the Broad Street Bridge, and they came from the streets of Regina. By the end of the month, the lake was holding more than a foot of water. It was still rising as March turned into April, and Wascana Lake was once again just that, a real lake.

photo by Roy Antal

*March 22, 2004, the last trip out of the lake bottom*

"Who would have thought that digging a hole would have caused such excitement?" said Ralph Goodale, the federal finance minister. "Together we have not only salvaged our beautiful lake from slow degradation, we've preserved and rebuilt the most precious asset at the heart of the largest and finest urban park in all of North America."

*photo by Bryan Schlosser*

*Water flows through the earthen dam near the Broad Street Bridge*

The people came to watch the final moments, to watch the equipment leave and to watch the water come roaring in. One who watched was Mirta Fonseca, who uses the park as a jogger. "I'm just so proud of this project. Out of 365 days a year, I use the park 200."

Everybody breathed a sigh of relief when it was over.

"There were a lot of doubters," said Dominion Construction vice-president Brian Barber. "It was a daunting task when we started on January 5th, but we got it done, and I applaud the work ethic of everybody involved."

Gord Broda, son of the founder of Broda Construction, Cas, was equally happy that the job was done right. "Broda Construction is extremely proud of the effort put forward by each and every one of our people. These guys toughed out some very ugly weather, some very difficult working conditions, to make this happen."

The lake was filling. But the job was far from complete. There was still the promenade alongside the Albert Street Bridge, the touching up of Pine Island, the waterfall, a fountain in the middle of the west side of the lake, a new launching area at the marina.

And the people who use Wascana Lake, the rowers, the canoeists, all those people who used to dread going onto the lake because of the weeds, could hardly wait to take the plunge in 2004.

*photo by Bryan Schlosser*

*It was a stunning sight watching the rock trucks leave for the last time*

*Work continues on
the new promenade bridge*

*photo by Don Healy*

*photo by Don Healy*

*photo by Paula Kuan*

*Soon, Wascana Lake was filled with activities*

*photos by Bryan Schlosser*

*photo by Charles Melnick*

# Chapter 10 The Guy in the Pit

Every day that I drove through Wascana Centre, I wondered what it was like for those guys from Broda Construction of Kamsack, Saskatchewan, which is where one of the most successful companies in this country got its start – with one lousy over-worked gravel truck. And, so, I went down there and I got one of the workers, on 12-hour shifts, and I talked to him about his job and about his life.

This is the column I wrote in March, after I left him alone so he could go back to the job he obviously loves.

**Danger
And drama
Down at
The lake**

THE PIT – It is in the afternoon, the sun is shining, the snow is turning to mush. Just off the front of the Legislative Building, there are people moving towards the big yellow dinosaur. Some of them are reaching for their cameras. Others are parking their cars where they are, jumping out, and joining those already there. They don't care about the parking tickets that may be slapped under their windshield wipers when they return.

What is this all about?

This is like some kind of a balancing act, and when you first see it, it takes your breath away and your stomach flutters. There is a pile of dirt, quite high, not all that big, sitting right in front of the legislative landing. And sitting on top of that pile of black dirt is one of those big yellow hoes. The kind that has the huge body and the long neck and can fill those rock trucks in what seems like the snap of a finger, the blinking of an eye.

The hoe, so big and yet so agile, is perched precariously close to the edge of this mountain of dirt as its operator in the cab moves the bucket deep into the soil, and scoops it back, as if building up the base. He is so close to the edge, you think, "One wrong move, and the whole thing will topple over."

*photo by Bryan Schlosser*

*They helped make it all possible*

Those are the adventurous moments of The Big Dig. As they surge towards the finish of this job, the conclusion of the deepening of the mighty Wascana, there are moments of defined drama such as that. The thing is, the drama reaches out and captures the imaginations of the people watching from the bridges, from the shores, from their vehicles. They perhaps see more than they are really seeing. But this is fun.

For those in the equipment, there is no drama. It is just another day at the office. The guys who are driving the rock trucks hauling away the dirt know what they are doing. This is nothing new to them. This is just another day at the office.

The guys laying the cement and sliding the pilings into the ground and building up the shores know what they are doing. It's just another day at the office. The guys sitting in the cabs of those giant hoes know what they're doing. It's just another day at the office for them.

I got an e-mail from somebody who jogs through Wascana Park every day and is in awe at what is happening. Each time, he sees progress. And from his watching all this stuff, he has embraced a deeply felt admiration for the job the guys in The Pit are doing. And, so, he has an idea. He wants a large rock placed somewhere along the shoreline. He wants upon that rock the names of every worker who was in The Pit and did this marvelous thing for our city. He wants only the workers' names. He does not want the politicians' names, he does not want the names of any government people. He wants only the names of the people who worked down there, 24 hours a day, seven days a week, so our city could be a better place. It is a wonderful idea, I hope they do it. This may well be another job to some people, just a bunch of heavy equipment hauling away dirt. But to the people who live in Regina, it has become far more than that. It has become an experience nobody will ever forget, and the idea of a huge rock with a plaque with names on it is a suitable tribute to something that was great. The Dig has made the guys working in the pit celebrities of a sort.

It has been such a project. From the very day all of this started, which was sometime in December, there has been this fascinating vigil from the shorelines of the lake. The routine is always the same down in The Pit. The big hoes reach into the ground and jerk up with a bucket full of dirt. The slow, deliberate, even graceful, movements of the hoes remind of the dinosaurs in the movies. The long neck moves out, then it bends, and goes down into the ground. The trucks back towards them, then stop, and the dirt is dumped in. In about two minutes the truck is loaded, and is off on its 15-minute return trip to one of the fill sites. They are hauling away 1.3-million cubic metres of dirt, and there are about 30 trucks, and they all operate 24 hours a day, seven days a week.

This is nothing new for Keith Bacon. He is from Prince Albert. He is 48 years old and he has been running this kind of equipment since 1973. He came into a trailer the other afternoon over by the SIAST campus, sat down in a chair, and talked about this life he leads. He had on a hard hat and the outfit he wears when he is operating the hoe. He is not a big man. His face is pleasant, weathered by the years working outside, his eyes are alive, his hands are strong. His uncle was the provincial superintendent of highways and that is how Keith Bacon was introduced to and came to love working with heavy equipment.

"I can run any of the equipment we've got here," he said. "I enjoy them all. And I enjoy the projects we work on. But the one I like the best is the hoe. There is a lot more activity with it and time goes faster. It's the busiest machine to be on. It can be tough sometimes. You have to have a plan. You have to know what you're doing and where you're going. You have to have a plan so you don't get boxed in."

I ask him, how many trucks can he load in one shift?

"Well, in 11 and one-half hours, I'll do about 240 loads."

Although Bacon has worked on jobs all over the country, some of them huge and some not so huge, and although he thought he had probably seen it all, this job in Wascana Lake is unique. "It's a bigger project," Bacon says, then smiles and his eyes light up. "There's lots of attention being paid to this job, lots of it, more than we've probably ever had. It's kind of surprising. We're definitely in the public eye. It's really just another job, but every time you look around, there are people on the shore and on the bridges watching. It doesn't matter if it's during the day, 10:30 at night, midnight or five in the morning, there is always somebody there watching."

His job is fascinating. The inside of the cab of a hoe looks like a spaceship. There are rows of dials. There are foot pedals and hand levers coming out of the floor that control the neck and the bucket. Not every guy off the street gets to operate one of these things. Remember, there is one hoe out there that costs $1-million and was brought to Regina from Belgium. The view from the hoe cab is clear, the operator able to see everything in front of him. "And," says Bacon, "you're up quite high." Only a couple of times has the hoe been stopped, both times by blizzards. "We could have kept going, but the guys in the trucks couldn't see where they were going."

Alternating between day and night schedules, Bacon works a 12-hour shift, from seven in the morning to seven at night, or the other way around, every day for two straight weeks at a time. Then, he gets a week off. It is the same for everybody in The Pit. Then, Keith Bacon gets a week off. It gives him a chance to go home to Prince Albert to visit his wife. They have three children, the oldest is Dale, who is 30 and who has been driving one of the rock trucks during The Big Dig. "We got married when I was 18," Bacon says, with a twinkle in his eyes, and then he chuckles, "I've still got my first wife."

The Big Dig. Skilled guys like him, who care so much about everything they do, that is why it is going so well.

photo by Bryan Schlosser

*The guys in The Pit*

# Chapter 11 Looking Back

In the days following the end of The Big Dig, veteran *Leader-Post* photographer Roy Antal went up in a small airplane and instructed the pilot to take him over Wascana Lake. He was on his way to a moment that may not be repeated for another 100 years, if ever. Antal wanted to capture this historic moment on film.

The plane stayed low to the ground as it headed east toward Wascana Centre. The pilot circled out over the Saskatchewan Centre of the Arts and there it was, laid out on the ground under the plane, a long, snaking line of rock trucks, excavators, graders. All the equipment that had been used in The Big Dig was traveling in a slow parade along the makeshift road that had been built at the bottom of the lake. They passed under the Broad Street Bridge, acknowledging the waves of the people who lined it and were watching in awe. The ground was still showing spots of snow when Antal snapped his photo of the last moments of those magnificent men and their awesome machinery at the bottom of Wascana Lake. They would never be back.

If the citizens of Regina had never seen anything like the display they had witnessed for about 80 days in the winter of 2004, then neither had the people who were down in The Pit, working at the job.

People came to Wascana Lake by the thousands, from the day The Big Dig started in early January to the day it ended in late March. They walked the shoreline of the lake, waving at the workers, taking pictures, bringing lunch for the workers, hanging signs off the Broad Street Bridge.

Brett Bertram of Prince Albert, a Broda excavator operator, remembers a single defining moment of what The Big Dig meant to the city, and thus to the workers. He was driving under the Broad Street Bridge when he glanced up. A young man had hung "Thank You" signs off the bridge. "Boy, did that make us feel good," said Bertram.

Mark Behrns, project manager for Dominion Construction, and Rusty Clunie, general manager of Broda Construction, were also caught off guard by all the interest in the project shown by the people of the city. They both figured there would be lots of interest at first, but that it would eventually disappear. They were happily wrong. Said Behrns, "People were really fascinated . . . What construction job would there be that would even warrant it?"

Behrns and Clunie found themselves in the media spotlight as the main spokesmen for what was going on during the dig. Clunie said the spotlight should have been pointed elsewhere. "It's really the people that worked day and night in the cold and doing everything who need the credit," he said.

*People stood and watched – some brought heartfelt signs of thanks*

*photos courtesy of Broda Construction*

*Rusty Clunie, Gord Broda, Paul Ochitwa, Brian Barber, Mark Behrns*
photos courtesy of Broda Construction

*Paul Ochitwa and Gord Broda*

photo by Don Healy
*Workers from Dominion Construction work on Pine Island*

*Wayne Clifton and Cas Broda*

*Robert Hellegards, Rob Broda, Norm Blunt, Rusty Clunie, Gord Broda, Cas Broda, Ed Kerluke*

The crews of Broda couldn't get over the attention they were receiving. "Everyone's taking your picture," recalled Brett Bertram.

Dale Bruce, a Broda foreman from Shellbrook, came to understand just how big the job was. He said it was like watching a child grow. You didn't notice the progress when you were on site each day. "But it was when you returned to The Pit after being away, you appreciated what had been achieved. It's a proud feeling. It's pretty awesome."

*photo by Don Mathieson*

*A beautiful spring day as the new lake fills*

Not long after the men and equipment of Broda had left, Wascana Lake began to fill, and soon there was more water in it than they wanted. The Miracle of Wascana Lake had been fulfilled. The people couldn't wait to get at it, nature's beautiful display right in the middle of a city surrounded by bald prairie.

There was a man who lived in Lakeview who wanted to be the first to take a canoe into the lake. But somebody got there before him. So, the man decided he would be the first to swim in the lake. And one Friday night he and his family went to its shores and he went into Wascana Lake and swam. Nobody knows for sure if he was the first, but it didn't really matter. He did it. He had waited all winter for that moment.

There was water, lots of it.

Everybody involved in the project had sweated it out, stomachs churning.

For Ray Pentland, a water resources engineer and consultant on the project, the worry was about how much spring runoff would there be, how much of it would reach the lake bottom, and when it would reach it.

The new lake holds about 2.5 billion litres of water, or nearly a thousand Lawson swimming pools. Pentland studied all the variables involved in how much water would be coming, and when. He looked at the highs and lows of flows to the average date of the spring runoff. The variations led to planning for all kinds of "what-if" scenarios.

"There was some risk involved that we were going to lose the project if the runoff started too soon," Pentland said. "But with this kind of job you had to take some risk or you'd never get it done."

Originally, the plan had been to spread the project over two years, but that was far too risky. "A stream like Wascana Creek occasionally has no flow at all for a whole year," explained Pentland. "It's very rare, but it has occurred several times in the record period, from the 1940s."

In the beginning of April, the lake was already about a metre deep because of the city runoff. Catchwater for about one third of the city – primarily the southeast neighbourhoods – spills into Wascana Lake. But the main water source is further upstream – rural runoffs from areas south and east of Regina along Wascana Creek, all the way out to Tyvan.

Mother Nature was not revealing her plans for when the spring runoff would come, or how much of it would actually make it to Regina. You can read historical data, plan, look at the moon, and pray, but the call will still be Mother Nature's to make.

The historical data indicated the average date of the spring runoff in Regina was March 29. But it can come any time between early March and mid to late April.

Mark Behrns summed it all up, put into one capsule comment why nerves were a little frayed as the work continued and the temperatures warmed.

"Here, the water comes, you're done," he said.

There were all sorts of contingency plans in place to cover every possibility. In the end, none of them were needed. The job was finished on schedule and Mother Nature waited until The Pit was emptied of men and machinery before she sent the water on its way.

Rusty Clunie said that it was very much a race against nature, "More than people know. We've won now."

*The making of Pine Island*

*photo by Roy Antal*

*photos by Don Mathieson*

*photo by Roy Antal*

Pine Island and the old Broad Street Bridge abutment – waiting for a waterfall

At the end of the day, the weather turned out to be The Big Dig's most pronounced obstacle.

"We always thought we'd be fighting with cold weather, not the warm weather that came in February and never left," said Behrns. When it all began, unseasonably warm temperatures in December kept the lake bed from freezing. After the dig got underway, work was shut down three times because of blizzards. January sent a wave of bitterly cold weather, the temperatures plunging well below zero, bottoming out at -55°C. Then, warmer weather made for greasy haul roads and mud-caked equipment. In the home stretch in March, it rained.

*Broda's workers never let up, or gave up*

photo by Murray Langgard

"It was a challenge," said Gord Broda, one of the owners of Broda Construction. "There were a few days there where we were wondering if Mother Nature was ever going to be nice to us."

The weather kept throwing curves at the crews from Broda and Dominion. While Broda's role was the digging, Dominion's centred around the enhancements, such as the Albert Street promenade, the pathway under the Broad Street Bridge, and the waterfall and walkway on Pine Island.

When the weather was bitterly cold, Broda's crews kept working. But Dominion's crews couldn't. Concrete work is out when it is -40°C and the wind is blowing. "You can't send men out in that kind of cold," said Behrns. Conversely, the warmer weather made it difficult for the concrete trucks to travel over the soft and slippery haul route. Therefore, much of the work had to be done in late evening or early morning when the frost was still on the road and the big cement trucks could travel safely.

*Spectators watch the deepening of the channel to Willow Island*

photo by Ken Jones

The weather wasn't the only bump in the road in The Big Dig.

There were a few other curve balls.

The initial tests conducted indicated that about 1.2-million cubic metres of earth would have to be taken out of the lake bottom. Fine. Broda could prepare its schedule for that. But in February, further tests were conducted and it became obvious that more dirt than the 1.2-million would have to be removed. The initial figure was based on sonar readings of the lake. However, the alluvium – the top layer of muck consisting of goose droppings, decayed vegetation and silt – was so saturated, the sonar mistook it for water. In reality, the alluvium was one or two metres deep in places – adding an extra 100,000 cubic metres to dig out.

At the same time, Saskatchewan Property Management Corporation decided, because of environmental concerns, not to have dirt from the The Pit trucked over to Goose Island, which is just east of the Saskatchewan Centre of the Arts. It was something that was allowed by federal permits, but SPMC made their decision in favor of the environment, despite increasing the work load and the costs.

Rusty Clunie explained. "Rather than getting the advantage of taking 200 to 250 thousand cubic metres half the distance (which would have saved time and fuel), I've had to run it all long, which was a big production feat because I've said from the day we got this job, with the 1.2-million, we'd have it done the third week of March. With those changes in place, we still achieved that under adverse conditions."

The extra dirt was sent the full length of the 4.5-kilometre haul road. Broda added five more trucks to its fleet of 22 to get the job done. In total, about 190,000 trips were made down the haul road.

*photo by Wesley Olson*
Prepping the south shoreline

The new south shoreline
*photo by Roy Antal*

The new north shoreline
*photo by Alan Lazarenko*

Soil problems also were encountered by Dominion's crews. Unstable soil by the Albert Street Bridge created a three-week delay when workers had to dig nearly a metre deeper than planned before filling it with concrete to make a foundation for the promenade.

At the opposite end of the west lake, the problem was reversed. Workers trying to install piles for the boardwalk at Pine Island hit nothing but rock. It cost them a week while they drilled through it.

None of the enhancements were completed by the time The Big Dig was over and the water came in. Work on those had always been scheduled to be handled over the summer and into the autumn.

As the summer of 2004 arrived, and the lake was filled with water, and people were using it, all of the problems that had surfaced from time to time during The Big Dig had vanished. The job was done, and now it was time for Reginans to make more memories of their times spent in Wascana Centre.

*photo by Alan Lazarenko*

*The grand opening of the new Wascana Lake*

On June 30, 2004, four smiling, giggling children put on their life jackets and jumped into Wascana Lake off the dock near the marina. It was something that hadn't been done for decades.

# Chapter 12  Memories

Wascana Centre means different things to different people. But there is one common bond – it is a place where memories are made. Memories of childhoods spent on the lake, or in the park. Memories of wedding pictures taken amongst the tall trees. Memories of boat rides and boat races. Memories of family picnics. Memories of Sunday afternoon walks. Memories of a lunch on a park bench. Memories of riding bikes along the paths. Memories of a stolen kiss on a moonlit night.

Wascana Centre can be all of the things you can imagine you would want in a park. When I began gathering material to write this book on not only The Big Dig, but the whole complex itself, I wanted to write it as much through the eyes of people who use the park as I could. So, in my column in the *Leader-Post*, I asked readers to send me their memories of their times in Wascana Centre. The response was terrific. So, here, in a book written for those who love Wascana Centre and all that it has brought to the enjoyment of the people of Regina, are the memories of some of those people who have taken the opportunity to look back with fondness and gratitude.

Enjoy . . .

On any day when the weather is decent, you can stroll through Wascana Centre and the view will always be the same. There will be people everywhere. Some will be walking the lakeshore. Others will be on their bikes, or roller blades, or running.

The picnic sites will be busy with families cooking their lunches on the open barbecues, blankets spread out on the thick green grass, the sweet smell of burning charcoal filling the air, children playing games nearby. You will find people quietly sitting on benches, looking out across the lake, enjoying themselves in the moment, soaking in the warmth, thinking.

And on the great lawns that are on each side of the Legislative Building and on the lawns in front of it can be found the boys and girls of summer. They will tossing Frisbees back and forth, the gentle arc of the saucers leading them on gallops across the grass, trying to reach out and snatch them before they spin into the ground. There will be people kicking soccer balls back and forth, or playing a lazy game of catch with a baseball.

Always, there will be a game of touch football. It has nearly always been there, at least for as long as I can remember.

I can remember the early days of my career with the *Leader-Post*, in the 1960s. Once a week, reporters, photographers and deskmen would head over to the legislative grounds. It would be later in the afternoon, when the day shift was ending and ours had yet to start. We always left sufficient time to permit us to head to the Regina Rams clubhouse after the games so as to receive some medical attention from Rams' trainers Jim Francis or Lloyd (Doc) Dobie. The games were so much fun, and the park was what made it that way. We would go to the field that is in front and to the west of the Legislative Building. We called it Scotty Melville Field, named after the then Sports Editor of the *Leader-Post*. The field was perfect for touch football. The grass was well kept and the field was level. It was surrounded by trees and the lake stretched out in front of us.

*picture by Josh Sawka*

*Touch football on the "Leg" lawn*

We played endless weeks of touch football there, some in the rain, the season ending with the falling of the first snowflakes. I was the quarterback for our team because I owned the ball. Talent had very little to do with that decision.

This was serious stuff. Sometimes, the games would become more than a little heated. I can recall one incident when one of reporters, Ken Cuthbertson, ticked off one of our deskmen from the sports department by, if I recall correctly, blocking him at the knees, which was a no-no. The deskman, Al Driver vowed to "get him."

The chance came. It should be mentioned that Cuthbertson was wearing a cast covering a dislocated thumb suffered in an earlier "friendly" game. The thumb had almost healed, but the cast had been kept on as a precautionary measure.

Cuthbertson's team had the ball. He came across the middle, looking for a pass. Driver was in the middle, covering him, and Driver saw his opportunity to get even for what Cuthbertson had done to him earlier. The ball was thrown. The pass was high. Cuthbertson left his feet to catch it. Driver, much taller, went with him and saw his chance. He could not hit Cuthbertson, that was clearly against the rules, and nobody wanted that.

But, as Cuthbertson went up, and as Driver went up, as their feet left the ground, it was as if everything was in slow motion. Driver saw something. He saw the cast on Cuthbertson's thumb. And as the ball arrived and Cuthbertson pushed his hand even further into the air to catch the ball, Driver's hand went straight for the cast, his eye-hand co-ordination had never been sharper. There was a snapping sound, witnesses reported, as the thumb was bent backwards. Cuthbertson fell to the turf, clutching his thumb and filling the air with his personal opinion of Driver. The invective continued as Cuthbertson walked off the field, in a huge sulk, to his car.

Rob Vanstone, the current sports columnist with the *Leader-Post*, and his group have continued the tradition of playing touch football on the "Leg" grounds. Columnists being wiser than the rest, Vanstone also plays quarterback, knowing that if you own the football, you have clout.

He recalls one game in the late 1990s in which his quarterbacking skills left something to be desired. "I was stinking and also limping around because my aged cleats were tearing up my feet. So, after the game, I decided to make a symbolic statement regarding my performance while ridding myself of the cleats. Therefore, I removed them, walked over to the edge of the lake, and threw them in the water. Glub, glub, glub . . ."

When Vanstone returned to the field, his football buddies were waiting for him.

"That's the first target you hit all day," chortled Mark Anderson.

And *Leader-Post* political columnist Murray Mandryk had only one observation to make. "Why did you untie the cleats before you threw them into the lake?"

Ah, the lazy hazy days of touch football in Wascana Centre.

# Memories

### By Jessie (Hibbs) Sellwood, Regina

My father, Dave Hibbs, came from England to Regina in 1905. After driving a bus at Fort San he was hired by Mr. Cook, who owned a house by the Power House (which is now the Science Centre).

Every morning my dad would get up at 5 o'clock, hitch up a team of horses, drive out to the Regina jail, pick up six or seven inmates and bring them back to Wascana Lake to plant trees. They worked six days a week. Each prisoner would get a package of rollings and papers (cigarettes). He would take them back to the jail in time for supper. This went on for two or three years.

*Saskatchewan Archives R-A6585-1*

*The early days on Wascana Lake*

*photo courtesy of City of Regina Archives B-779.1*

*Picknicking and boating on Wascana Lake ca. 1913*

# Memories

### by E. Pearl O'Byrne, Regina

My memory takes me back to the 1920s. Since I was born in 1916, my memories are those of a young child in the 1920s, seven or eight years old. I was the youngest of a large family that often had a picnic in the park on Sunday afternoon – a fun time for all. It was an era when only the wealthy owned a car. I remember my mother packing a picnic lunch and all of us traveling by streetcar to the park. The streetcar ran on tracks down the middle of the street as far south on Albert Street to Campion College.

We went swimming in the lake. I remember the wooden change rooms, then running out onto the wooden pier, and jumping off the end. I couldn't swim at that time but I had a lot of fun trying. Then, my brothers played catch ball. I remember concerts played by the Salvation Army Band in the bandstand.

Our picnics were usually on the north side of the lake. But one memory is of my teenaged brother taking me to climb the stairs to the top of the Legislative Building to a small open-air structure where we could see over the city. My brother disappeared. How was I to find my mother? I was very frightened. He was playing a trick on his kid sister. I never went again. I think the structure is closed to the public now.

*Saskatchewan Archives R-B674*

*The ladies go for a swim in the lake*

Under no circumstances should a fast-food outlet be allowed to do business in the park. The beauty and serenity of the park is indeed a jewel for the people to enjoy.

Fast forward to my early experience as a grandmother. Two young grandchildren, ages seven and four, were in my care one winter due to a family breakup. Waskimo was indeed a blessing. The children had fun as they watched and participated in some of the activities. Winter in the park is very much a play time, too. Even Grampa and Gramma later purchased skis for cross-country skiing. Lessons were given in the park. As the years advanced our fun on skis became very limited. The children grew up and as adults soon learned to use our skis. Waskimo is indeed a happy memory.

# Memories

### By Elsie Hughes Shepherd, Regina

Back in 1927, after my mother, Sarah, my brothers Arthur and Leslie and I had moved from our home in Winnipeg to Regina to help my cousins and their recently widowed father, William, cope with their suddenly changed lives, I was an adventuresome girl of eight. My oldest cousin, called Billy, was also eight. We became great pals. Billy was my closest friend in those days.

At the time, we lived at 682 Albert Street, in a house long since a part of the history of Regina's growing years. I think the day I remember was probably a hot summer's day. My mother – doubtless wanting us to stop being rambunctious in the house – gave Billy and me a whole nickel each. What a prize! We could either spend it on some glorious treat of candy or we could take the streetcar south down Albert Street to Wascana Park and the lake for a swim in its cooling waters.

As much then as today, I loved eating sweets. Billy must have felt the same. We had a hard decision to make. We clutched the silver coins in our hands then thrust them back into our pockets, grabbed some gear for swimming and headed out on a long 20-block journey. Along the way, we stopped to watch some men constructing a couple of new buildings – McGavin's Bakery and the Adanac Brewery.

At the corner of 11th Avenue and Albert Street, we hurried into the Saskatchewan Co-op Creamery where Uncle William was a supervisor. He gave us a personal tour of the plant and then treated us each to an Eskimo pie, a delicious ice-cream sandwich. We walked and talked our way to the beautiful park, then only a few blocks away.

When we reached Wascana Park, we quickly changed into our swimming costumes in the bathhouse and left our street clothes (and those precious coins) in a locker. We frolicked and played in the water – I can still remember sliding off the pier that extended from the grassy shore into the mighty Wascana.

*Saskatchewan Archives R-B13146*

*Swimming and sailing in the good old days*

After lots of giggles and horseplay – and probably more than one mouthful of lake water, we had to wend our weary way home. We glumly dried ourselves and changed back into our street clothes and started the long trek home. And then we remembered the fortune we had – and it truly was a fortune to a couple of kids in the pre-Depression days of 1927! We bought some yummy treats and, energized by the memory of the swim, we made it home and ended another prairie childhood day.

Wascana Lake, all blue and sparkly in the sun, looking up at the Legislative Building beyond on the south shore, was a magnificent place back then – an escape for everyone from the drudgeries of work. And that day – probably because of my cousin Billy and me having so much fun together – has remained as clear with me after all these years as it was when it really happened.

My mother, Sarah Hughes, was a strong-willed woman. Known as Sadie to her many friends and colleagues, mother worked at the Legislative Building in the provincial laboratories. It was a good healthy walk from our apartment in the Donohue Block on the north side of 11th Avenue, between Smith and Lorne Streets. We had moved there from my uncle's house at 682 Albert Street.

Mother could walk south on Smith or any of the other streets that led her toward Wascana Park and the lake, which fronted the imposing Legislative Building. In the dreary winter months, rather than heading west to Albert Street and walking across the bridge, mother would strike a path across the frozen surface of the silent Wascana. Wrapped up in a big fur coat to fight the blasts of the weather, she thought she was ready for any climactic assault.

Well, one day in the winter of 1934 or 1935, her jaw doubtlessly firm with characteristic "Sadie determination," mother set forth on her daily march. Alas, the weather had warmed and the ice on the lake had started to shift and crack. It gave way, and mother – great coat and all – fell into the frigid and murky waters. Perhaps buoyed by the coat, perhaps buoyed by her determination, but she was most definitely buoyed by a faith that her life was not going to be swallowed up by some man-made, dug-out lake in the middle of some Canadian prairie town. Not likely for this woman, far from her Belfast home, was this temporary inconvenience going to be the "the end".

*Saskatchewan History and Folklore Society – Everett Baker Collection*

*Harvesting ice from Wascana Lake in 1940s – the blocks were sold to restaurants and households in the days before refrigerators*

A group of young men, gathered at the nearby Regina Boat Club, another long-lost ghost of the past, had been standing on the verandah watching mother trundle across the icy expanse. In horror, they saw her topple through an ever-widening fissure. They rushed to her rescue, saving not only mother but also that heavy, soggy coat.

Mother was whisked away to hospital where she convalesced for some time. I had to leave school to work as there was no short-term or long-term disability coverage in those days. I was about 15 at the time.

*photo courtesy of Grant Mcdonald*
*Legislative Building circa 1920*

I remember that when we were teenagers, the boys would like to take the girls out on the waters of the Wascana. They would rent canoes or small boats and treat us to romantic rides. A favourite destination was Willow Island.

I also remember families and young people taking rides on a paddle boat which offered an hour float on the lake. That was around the time of the war.

I remember people taking their cars down to wash them along the Broad Street shore in the 1950s. But people always went to the park for picnics and family outings.

*Saskatchewan Archives R-B9513*
*Vintage cars parked in front of the Legislative Building – at the time, they were the latest models*

# Memories

BY AGNES LESLIE, PRINCE GEORGE, B.C.

*A diving platform in Wascana Lake*

In the 1930s and early 1940s Wascana Lake and Wascana Park were the only place where the proverbial "gangs" would hang out. We had a real nice group. There were my brothers Ed and Bob, and friends Buster, Peter, Rudy, Cec and Joe. The girls were Eva, Mary, Helen, Josie and myself. We were always together and planned our events together, except when we girls would trudge off on a Saturday morning to go swimming, because the dressing room was open and the boys would try to look in. We would never tell them we were going, but somehow they seemed to find out. We would spend hours wading around in water waist deep. We would not dare venture further so I never did know how deep the lake was. There was a lifeguard and he would blow the whistle if we ventured out too far. We would bring lunch and lie on the green grass and munch away and tell all our deepest secrets. It was a glorious time and summers were filled with these outings.

Sundays we would go to the park after supper. There was a large round bandstand in the open part of the park and the boys brought their guitars, mouth organs or whatever. We would sing along with the crowds of people that would group around the bandstand. Of course, the local bands would play on the bandstand too.

At that time in Regina, the Burns company had a big high tank on top of a large high stand. The whistle would blow at 9 p.m., which meant all of us had to go home and clear the park as the music and fun were over.

We would hike around the park and have scavenger hunts during the summers. Oh, those summers were magic.

In the 1940s the war was on. A lot of men in Regina had signed up for the air force, the army or navy. So at age 19 there was not much left for good "pickin". We girls decided to join the YWCA and meet some of the military who would come to the YWCA to socialize. One of the things we were not to do was give our last names or phone numbers in the event that we would become too friendly. The place was supposed to be for military men, but the girls belonged to the YWCA.

It happened that my friend was in the naval attachment (HMCS Queen) and was stationed on Wascana Lake in the barrack which he called "The Stone Frigate". Many a night we went skating on the lake, then walked home to a sip of cocoa and sandwiches which my mother had made for us.

It was a treat when the moon was out and shone on the lake. There is nothing like a harvest moon in Saskatchewan – sure makes one feel romantic.

I remember the weeds, but we got used to that.

Those were the lazy, hazy days of summer and the mysterious days of winter where we would practically know just about everyone that came to the park, and there was no fear of anyone hurting you or making your stay there scary. We felt free and trustful.

I left Regina a long time ago, but when I came back and drove down Albert Street and saw the bridges and Wascana Park so lovely and green and well kept, I said to myself, "That was really a lovely place when I was young, and it still is, perhaps now more than ever."

*Saskatchewan History and Folklore Society – Everett Baker Collection*

*What better way to spend a Sunday afternoon than in the lake – 1940s*

# Memories

BY SHARON PENNER, MOOSE JAW

My sister and I were fortunate to have Wascana Park as our backyard while growing up. We lived with our parents and grandparents in one of the four beautiful two-storey houses in the grounds which have since been torn down. There were children of all ages in the four homes. Ours was the "S.E. Cottage" and was reserved for the chief engineer of the Government Power House (my grandfather G. Ernest Stuhr). The S.W. Cottage was the home of the Chief Electrician and his wife, Doug and May Newbury. Inge and Ernie Park, the Chief Gardner, lived in the N.W. Cottage (before Joe Moran) and in the N.E. Cottage was the Chief Painter, Bernard Hartnell, and his wife, Isabel. I lived there from 1946 to 1953.

All the way from Albert Street (at McCallum Avenue) to the four houses, there was a wooden sidewalk, which would be seething with worms during a rain. On those days Mom could always expect us home from school earlier because Sandra (my sister) would chase me with one or two worms dangling from her hand.

During the deep cold of winter it was eerie and a little frightening to walk along the sidewalk and hear tree branches snapping with the cold. In high school, I had a potential boyfriend who insisted I meet him at Albert Street rather than him coming to the house to get me. He was afraid of the park at night. Needless to say, that romance went nowhere.

*Saskatchewan Archives R-B8732*

*Tennis was the game of choice on the north shore*

*Saskatchewan Archives R-A3739-3*

*The lake was a great place for skating in the beginning and . . .*

Speaking of romance, we loved checking out the cars parked around the park with couples necking. Then we'd pound a couple of times on the trunk, holler and run. Never did get caught!

If the shale box at the tennis court was almost empty, we would crawl through the box, into the court and play a little tennis.

Throughout the summer, there was always an RCMP constable (in red serge) on horseback patrolling the grounds and available for photo ops with visitors.

The flower beds were planted and tended by prisoners from the jail. I don't know if they did other jobs around the park but they did the flowers, including the flower beds in our yards.

In the winter, Mr. Park always flooded a skating rink in his vegetable garden for us. Since I was the aspiring figure skater, I would train the others in skating routines for our own ice show. We would make posters and slap them up everywhere between the grounds and Lakeview School. Mrs. Park helped with the sound system.

During summer holidays we would put on our own circus. I remember telling fortunes as a gypsy one year, which was a whole lot safer than the springboard act we tried another year. David Park jumped off the window sill of the Power House onto a teeter-totter set-up where I was standing on the far end. I was to gracefully go into the air and come back down gracefully, landing on my feet. Instead, I had a broken coccyx, which bothered me for years. We also had our own concession stand – my mom made hot dogs and cut them into smaller bits so they could be sold for 5 cents.

We were so fortunate to have Wascana Park as our backyard.

*photo by Josh Sawka*

*. . . it still is!*

# Memories

BY GREGG HALLSWORTH, REGINA BEACH

I am a child of the Fifties who lived in the 2500 block of Winnipeg Street, just three blocks north of the Power House, where my father worked as an electrician for over 30 years. My dad, Jesse, his siblings and parents, Samuel and Gertrude Hallsworth, arrived in Regina from Moose Jaw in 1910. Grandad was a blacksmith for the CPR, having made thousands of iron hoops that held together the wooden pipeline from the water wells northeast of the city. They lived in the 1200 block of Rae Street, receiving a direct hit from the terrible tornado of 1912. My mom, Patricia (Greenaway) Hallsworth, also had early roots in the history of Regina. Her dad, Ed, operated Greenaway's Lunch on 11th Avenue and her uncle Russ and his son, Ken Reid, operated R and K's Lunch on Hamilton Street. My mother still remembers the 1931 excavation of Wascana Lake – unfortunately, we have no pictures of the event.

As a child, I was always warned by my parents about the dangers of playing at Wascana Lake near the Power House. Being a typical kid, this was the first place my buddies and I frequented, despite the consequences of being detected. We began by playing in a sheltered area just west of the Power House, before the park was developed there. Luckily, my dad never saw us, or our adventures would have abruptly been cut short. The first "hangout" was an area where old four-foot-diameter concrete storm sewer drain pipes had been dumped at the edge of the lake, helter-skelter. Some were on their ends and full of soil, some on their sides, making convenient little islands with stepping-stone-like access. This created the perfect place for us kids to play "knights and castles" or to scoop up the frogs and minnows that called the area among the bulrushes home. At one point, a buddy slipped off one of the pipes, sinking his feet into the shallow water and good old Wascana muck. A quick trip through the lawn sprinkler at home to wash off the goop, to honestly be able to say he had been playing in the lawn sprinkler, rather than being down at the lake, got him a "cuff on the ear" – a small punishment for a much larger crime.

Once the concrete pipe area lost our interest, we wandered further west along the lake, playing in the few natural areas of bushes or just kicking leftover buffalo bones in the dirt as we conquered yet more territory. By the time we reached Grade 7, during the mid-1960s, we would visit the same area, with permission from our parents, as it was being developed into the beautiful parkland it is now. We would have picnic lunches, watching the area being developed and landscaped and playing for hours among the lawn sprinklers.

My brothers and their friends introduced us to another delight of Wascana Park – the bicycle paths. They ran from the Broad Street Bridge (the old steel bridge) around the south side of the lake, roughly following the spiffy new paved pathway developed in 2003, from the bridge abutment to the Legislative Building. I'm sure there were paths I don't remember. Many times, we saw people fishing on the east side of the north bridge abutment just about where the marina is today, under the shade of huge pines, cottonwoods and willows, catching an enviable string of pike for supper – a real treat for us "East Enders".

*The old Broad Street Bridge*  *Saskatchewan Archives R-16789-1*

Sometime during the early 1960s, the Broad Street Bridge gave us another challenge – walking right under it on the lake bottom from the east side, nearly to Willow Island, when the lake dried up during a drought. The bottom of the lake at that time was composed of large 'tiles" of dried goop (a combination of prairie gumbo and goose poop) with big cracks between them, baked in the hot sun of those dry years. We walked from one tile to another nearly to the island, until they became wet and unstable, like potter's clay, where they would no longer hold our weight.

We also enjoyed several happy parent-approved walking excursions to the Museum of Natural History and to the Legislative Buildings. I'm sure my parents, who enjoyed a long history in the arts of the city, including the Regina Symphony Orchestra, were pleased to see their kids interested in such things. It was a thrill to climb the hundreds of stairs to the top of the Legislative Building to peer down at the flower beds that are still so beautiful. They looked like majestic Persian rugs that could fly you on all kinds of childhood trips. Or we would marvel at the green-coloured lake below, in wonder at where we'd played.

It was only a short time ago that I went through the now "Royal" Saskatchewan Museum and was absolutely so proud to show its new elegance to guests from the Yukon, who marveled at its majesty. Later, they were amazed how we could sit in the then Park Place Restaurant and feel as if we were at a country resort rather than in the heart of the Capital City.

The excitement of The Big Dig has once again piqued my interest and revived some of my most cherished childhood memories. Best of all, there still remains one of the bastions of happy childhood times at Wascana Lake – the old Broad Street Bridge abutment. I always look for its unmistakable shape.

# MEMORIES

### BY DR. MARK DOWHANIUK, TORONTO, ONTARIO

I was born in Regina in 1968 and lived there until I moved to Toronto in 1990. My family moved to 3047 Quinn Drive in the spring of 1972. Quinn Drive runs east off of Broad Street, just north of the Broad Street Bridge. The house had a unique design with a lot of glass windows facing south. What really attracted my parents was the big backyard, but that was not all. Through the back gate and across the lane, our backyard extended into Wascana Park. When I tell my wife and children stories of my childhood, they almost always include memories of Wascana Park and Wascana Lake.

Most people who have never been to Regina have a certain impression of the Queen City that does not include the beautiful expansive parkland that is Wascana Park. If only Toronto could be so fortunate.

Much of my childhood was spent exploring the park with my brother Pete and my best friend Ron Osterried, who also lived on Quinn Drive. One of my earliest childhood memories of Wascana Lake was riding in a rubber dingy with my father and his friend Gary. My father had a large and seemingly sturdy rubber dingy and somehow he and Gary managed to paddle Pete and me over to the old Broad Street Bridge abutment. As we looked up, we noticed a group of teenagers sitting on the edge eating Kentucky Fried Chicken. Someone yelled down and asked if we wanted a piece of chicken. It was late afternoon and my brother and I were really hungry so we could not believe our luck. The first piece landed in the water and I remember picturing some huge fish swallowing the piece whole. The second piece landed in the boat and, much to my chagrin, my father awarded the younger son the first piece of booty. I remember a long pause and worrying that I would go hungry. Then another piece landed on the boat, bounced, and was retrieved by my father. I then proceeded to chew every last piece of meat from the bone.

During the elementary school years, we spent many weekends canoeing on the lake. Early Saturday morning, my father would haul the canoe through the backyard, across Wascana parkway, and down to the lake. Peter, Ron and I would carry the life jackets and the paddles. For some reason, we were afraid the police would arrest us for carrying a canoe through the park, so we would work quickly. Once the marina was built, we would drive the short distance and launch the boat from there. We liked to head east toward the old power station and the bird nests. To us it always seemed like wild unexplored territory. The east side of the lake near the Centre of the Arts was always my favourite spot. There was rarely anyone around, except for the birds and the beer bottles. Later in the summer, the weeds would be so high and thick that our canoe acted more like a gondola, requiring a push off the weeds as opposed to the conventional way of rowing.

Other times we would travel to the more inhabited west side of the lake towards the Legislature. To get there, we had to travel under the Broad Street Bridge. This always seemed like a harrowing death-defying feat. First, there was the rumbling of the cars above that echoed underneath. Then there was the narrow cement ledge five inches above the water on the side of the bridge, requiring a small portage. We would empty everyone from the canoe and stand on the ledge while my father lifted the canoe over the ledge to the other side. Then, one by one, we slowly and carefully got back into the canoe and travelled, west toward

*Saskatchewan History and Folklore Society – Everett Baker Collection*
*Making the pleasant journey to Willow Island in a sternwheeler in the 1940s*

Spruce Island. Other than a few empty beer bottles, Spruce Island was uninhabited and was quickly claimed as OUR island. I remember the ferries, Wasca I and Wasca II, that transported the picnic crowds from the mainland to Willow Island, which was not our favourite place to be because that was where all the people were.

We always returned from our canoe trips carrying more out than we carried in. I wonder just how much money we made on all the beer bottles we fished out of the lake and off the islands.

Living in downtown Regina, I grew to appreciate how lucky I was growing up where I did. Even my friends in Regina did not have the experiences that Ron, Peter and I had living so close to the lake. My family and I recently bought a house in Etobicoke. We have a big backyard and beyond the fence there is a ravine/park with a river running through it. Hopefully, our children can get a sense of what it was like for me growing up in Regina with Wascana Park and Wascana Lake as my backyard.

I look forward to seeing the newly renovated lake. I expect the old aroma of algae and more algae is gone. I am probably the only person nostalgic for the smell of Wascana Lake.

# Memories

BY LINDA SHINMURA, REGINA

The Regina Japanese-Canadian Club moved its annual picnic from Boggy Creek in King's Park to the Goose Hill in Wascana Park in 1977, and it has been held there ever since. This picnic is an opportunity for the members of the Japanese-Canadian community, along with temporary residents and visitors from Japan, to get together and socialize in the magnificent setting provided by the greenery of Wascana.

Traditionally, on a Sunday in June, each family packs a picnic basket with a mixture of Japanese and Canadian goodies, and everyone gathers at the park for the noon meal. This is followed by an afternoon filled with activities such as novelty races and ball games. Club funds take care of some of the expenses, but we invariably have generous member donations of ice cream, watermelon, prizes and other treats. In the early evening, everyone pitches in to put together a barbecue.

This event is a tradition enjoyed by all age groups, toddlers to seniors, and we hope it will long outlive us, as will the park itself.

*photo courtesy of Wascana Centre Authority*

*Picnicking in the park*

# Memories

### by Chris Brewer, Regina Beach

I am the CEO of the Saskatchewan Snowmobile Association. Last November, I was contacted by a salesman from Kramer Ltd. and asked about the Last Mountain Lake Drifters Snowmobile Club at Regina Beach. I happen to be involved with the Drifters. The salesman inquired about the Drifters' grooming equipment and the cost to rent our groomer.

I provided him with our costs. I then contacted Brian Barber, vice-president of Dominion Construction. I have known Brian for a long time and we are long-time friends. Brian and I discussed what Kramer was looking for and Brian put me in touch with Gord Broda. Gord and I talked about renting the club's groomer and he chose to deal directly with the Drifters. Mr. Broda and I came to terms on price and responsibility of any damage. Mr. Broda required the machine that day and he sent a truck to pick up the unit. I agreed to come in to test if this would be the outcome we required. Broda was wanting to pack the snow cover to get frost into the ground to host the weight of his large equipment, to start The Big Dig on time. Broda could not start the project without a required frost depth and a little snowmobile club from Regina Beach could provide the assistance to help get The Big Dig started. In fact, the first piece of equipment on the dig area was from a little snowmobile club from Regina Beach. The machine arrived at Wascana and I met Mr. Broda. I unloaded the machine from the semi-trailer, let it warm up, and asked Mr. Broda if he cared to join me on the maiden voyage out onto the mighty Wascana. I must tell you we had been told by Wascana Centre that the lake was drained. Well, Broda and I proceeded onto the lake, close to the Broad Street Bridge. Things looked good, we bladed some snow and the machine floated over the mud very well.

photo by Roy Antal

*This tractor didn't go too far*

Broda said to me, "Let's try the outer side of the lake." So we went across the channel to the north. We got about halfway and down went the groomer into water, just covering the tracks. I revved the motor and backed out of the water onto safe ice. At this time, I informed Broda that the machine should go to the shop to dry and be checked over. Broda agreed and we made arrangements with Dave Wellings to put the machine in his shop for the night. The next day the machine checked out okay and we returned to Wascana. I met with Gord Broda and we attacked the project from a different perspective. "Let's check where the water is and avoid this problem until the river channel is pumped out." Things worked well and I trained an operator from Broda Construction. He would operate the machine on the weekend as I was away on business. On Saturday, November 22nd, I was in Yorkton at a groomer operators' training course. I received a call from Brian Barber just as the course was winding up. Brian informed me the groomer had broken through the ice just west of the old Broad Street Bridge abutment, and he wanted to know how long it would be before I returned to Regina.

I informed Brian I would return immediately. Brian informed me he was arranging for a crane and a semi-trailer to load the groomer on, and where we would take the machine to repair any damage. When I arrived about an hour and a half later, the crane was setting up and the truck had not yet arrived. I walked over to the bank and saw that the groomer was in about four feet of muck and goose droppings. The crane hoisted the groomer out of the lake onto the truck and off to Kramer Ltd. Gord Broda called from Prince Albert and asked for Kramer to work on the machine for the remainder of the weekend and to keep them on it so as to get back on Wascana Lake as soon as possible.

The following Wednesday, the groomer returned to Wascana with the Drifters' operator, Chad Fink, as operator. It continued to work on the lake until mid-January of 2004. Farm tractors started to pull the larger tractors over the lake bed where the groomer had helped create the required frost. Thanks to Brian Barber and Gord Broda, a little snowmobile club from Regina Beach was able to make the kind of contribution that may have helped The Big Dig start on time.

photo by Roy Antal

*Grooming and prepping for The Big Dig*

photo by Roy Antal

*Not quite frozen!*

*Saskatchewan Archives R-A2883-3*
*The view from the top of the Legislative Building looking north –*
*Albert Street Bridge and the old Wascana Winter Club at the left in the 1940s*

# Chapter 13 In the end, Regina won

It was midway through the afternoon of the first day of autumn and the leaves on the trees that so dominate Wascana Centre were turning colour. The lead grey skies, the mist, the seeping clouds of the last day of summer had been whisked away by the fall wind and the sky was now that incomparable Saskatchewan blue, sprinkled with a few popcorn puffs of clouds. The fall colours of orange and yellow, and even some red, blended together. From the far side of Wascana Lake, the south side, they presented yet another picture of the park Reginans have come to love and visitors have come to admire.

The autumn season can be the most beautiful of all in Wascana Centre. This year, 2004, it seemed to take on a different, deeper texture. The lake, the new fountain spraying high into the air with the wind bending its plumes, the shoreline, the changing colours of the leaves that were so dense because of all the moisture, brought Wascana Centre to life as never before.

The orange fence that once had ringed the whole lake to keep people out now could be found only at the west end of the lake, at the promenade, and guarding the newly created Pine Island. Work was still going on in both places. In the mid-afternoon of the first day of autumn, the activity had picked up in both places as the completion date of the end of November neared. There were small back hoes, a grader or two, large tubes of pipe sitting in piles by cement structures – all waiting to be put into the ground near the promenade. The promenade, when finished, will end the need for people to make what can be a dangerous journey along a narrow sidewalk on the Albert Street Bridge from the north side of the lake to the south side. There never has been enough room on that bridge for walkers, people pushing baby strollers, people riding bikes and people running. The promenade will make it much easier, much safer and, certainly, a much more enjoyable stroll.

photo by Arnold McKenzie

*The new fountain helps aerate the lake and adds to the majesty of the Legislative grounds*

The activity on Pine Island was similar in its briskness. Pine Island was carved out of land that once had a road leading onto the old Broad Street Bridge. Now, it is an island unto itself, and, oh, when the work on it is finished what a glorious addition it will be to Wascana Centre. The plan calls for a walkway around the west side, and then behind a 4.25 metre waterfall created from the old Broad Street Bridge abutment. A footbridge to carry people from the main shore onto Pine Island is already in place.

The autumn is a time of year when Wascana Centre comes alive. If you venture over to the east lake, the activity is incredible. Hundreds of birds of all kinds can be found gathering in the shallow waters, not just the usual Canada geese, but all kinds. They are using the centre as a stopping point, a resting spot, a gathering place for the migration south, and every once in a while there is a rare sighting which excites the bird enthusiasts. On the west side of the lake are 20 or so pelicans, great white birds which have been around the lake for most of the summer, the largest number of pelicans I have ever seen here. The noise from the birds is constant in the autumn, carrying through the thin air as they trumpet the end to their summer in the north country. At dusk, it grows even louder and carries even further across the city because that is when the geese leave the park to snack on what they can find in the farmers' fields on the outskirts of Regina.

Autumn is a great time to go into the park. And it was even greater in the autumn of 2004 because everything seemed so much better, so much richer, so much more intense. This was largely because now the lake had more body, more presence. It looked like a real lake. And everything around it looked better. The Big Dig had done its job.

photo by Roy Antal

*In the autumn of the year 2004 the lake was a busy place*

*photo by Roy Antal*

*A great park in the middle of a great city*

On the first day of autumn, a man was busy putting up a colourful sign at the entrance to the park off Broad Street, near the marina. The sign read: "The Willow on Wascana." It was now official. Wascana Centre's latest restaurant venture was ready to let the world know it was there. Again, a restaurant was opening on the shores of the mighty Wascana, in the small comfortable building located on the southeast shore, presenting diners with a spectacular view of the west side of the lake. At night, it's a stunning place to enjoy a fine-dining experience.

The Willow on Wascana opened in August of 2004, taking over from Park Place which, despite an appealing menu, wasn't able to make a go of it. A handful of local restaurant people have opened the Willow and they will be keying on the lunch and dinner patrons that keep the hundreds of Regina restaurants busy year round. There is no other restaurant in Regina that offers the view The Willow does. If its popularity in the beginning is an indication, then it does seem to have a solid future. It is a very pleasant place, an open floor plan, great views, plenty of wood, terrific atmosphere.

The timing for The Willow on Wascana could not be better. It fits in perfectly with what has been the theme of 2004 in the life of Wascana Centre. A new look to an old friend. That is what has happened to this park. It is not just a paint job either, a makeover if you will. It is the real deal. It has been regenerated, reborn with substance and soul.

This city did something in 2004 that stretched the imagination and stirred the soul. It kept alive, burning brightly and strongly, the prairie torch of optimism and resilience that has served our city so well for all these years. When Regina's forefathers arrived, there was nothing but barren prairie and endless wind, with a wisp of a creek winding through. Applying foresight, dreams and a perseverance beyond imagining, it has become a beautiful city with its own incomparable park, its own magnificent lake, its own secure shelter from the trials of daily life – accessible to everyone. Regina did it all by itself, literally taking nothing and creating a masterpiece.

There is still the endless wind. But now it whistles through the thousands of trees that have been planted, blowing through the branches and moving across a lake that now has real depth, a depth that allows the wind to create genuine waves.

Wascana Centre is indeed the prize jewel in Regina's crown. Reginans would have it no other way.

*Regina's prize jewel at night*

*photo by Clara Chief*

# The Big Dig – Facts & Figures

| | |
|---|---|
| *October 3, 2003* | The federal, provincial and municipal governments announced an $18-million project to deepen Wascana Lake |
| *October, 2003* | Gates opened at the Albert Street Bridge to drain lake |
| *November 30 – December 15, 2003* | Construction of the haul road along the lake bed using soil from Wascana Hill |
| *January 6, 2004* | Digging started |
| *March 18, 2004* | The promenade deck at the Albert Street Bridge was lowered by crane in four large preconstructed sections |
| *March 21, 2004* | Excavation of lake completed |
| *March 26, 2004* | Spring runoff released into lake |
| *March 28, 2004* | Excavation ceremony attended by thousands of people |
| *November 2004* | Completion date for the project |

## BIG DIG FINDS:

When the lake was drained in October, contractors found five bicycles, two bathtubs, one park bench, 27 beer bottles, 20 sandbags, one canoe, one Walkman, one radio and seven tires.

## BIG DIG ISLANDS:

Willow and Spruce Islands, originally created from the fill shovelled from the lake in 1931, grew by 20 and 30 per cent respectively.

Pine Island, formed from the old Broad Street Bridge abutment, is one of the recreational enhancements to the lake.

## EQUIPMENT:

Dominion Construction was the contractor; Broda Construction was the sub-contractor.

The rock trucks made approximately 156,000 one-way trips, amounting to 1,012,000 kilometres. The haul to the furthest fill area was approximately 4.6 kilometres.

## TYPE OF EQUIPMENT

1 1983 TEREX TS14B Motorscraper
3 1990 CAT 631E Motorscrapers
1 1997 CAT D10R Crawler Tractor (push)
1 1997 CAT D9R Crawler Tractor (push)
1 1997 CAT D9N Crawler Tractor (push)
1 1991 CAT D8N (earth, push)
1 1998 CAT D8N (earth, push)
1 1993 CAT D8N (earth, push)
3 1997 CAT D6M LGP Crawler Tractor
3 1989 CAT 16G Graders (Earth Operation)
6 1997 CAT D300E Rock Trucks
17 1992 - 1996 CAT Rock Trucks 773B
3 1992 - 1996 CAT Rock Trucks 769C
1 1997 CAT 345B L Excavator
3 1998 CAT 330B L Excavator
1 1989 CAT 235 C Excavator
2 1990 Komatsu WA-600 Loaders
1 1992 CAT 988B Loader
1 1998 Komatsu PC -750 Excavator – This was the second largest mass excavator with a bucket capacity of 7 cubic yards
1 2004 CAT 385 BL 8yd3 Excavator – This large mass excavator has a bucket capacity of 8 cubic yards. The Caterpillar mass excavator, one of the biggest of its kind in the world, weighed in at more than 90,000 kilograms and could fill a regular sized truck in just three scoops.

### COMPACTION:

1 815B Padfoot
1 Tractor c/w sheepsfoot

## DIRT

According to Mark Behrns, project manager with Dominion Construction: Originally an estimated 1.2 million cubic metres of earth would have to be moved but, in fact, 1,327,600 cubic metres was moved from the lake. There was an additional cut from the bottom of the lake, however, that material was used for shore treatments so it was not technically moved from the lake. Also 126,400 cubic metres of topsoil was stripped off the stockpile sites. That brings the total amount of dirt moved into the 1,540,000 range.

The average amount of dirt moved per day was 19,000 cubic metres.

## WATER

According to Ray Pentland, Wascana Centre Authority hydrologist: The last survey of the entire lake from Albert Street to the marsh east of the bypass was completed in 1990. Then capacity was roughly 1,500 cubic decametres (1.5 billion litres) – down about 12 per cent from a similar survey in 1962 due to sediment accumulation. Presumably the 1962 survey was also down from the volume contained in the lake after the 1930s work and down from the original 1908 volume, but good surveys are unavailable. The final volume is about 2,500 cubic decametres (2.5 billion litres).

## FUEL

Approximately 3.5 million litres of fuel was used at a cost of about $2.2 million.

# MANPOWER

## DOMINION CONSTRUCTION

Rick Balch
Joel Bancescue
Shane Bancescue
Brian Barber
Nick Beckett
Mark Behrns
Allan Cullen
Art Daigneault
Ken Ferguson
Byron Glover
Eugene Hamilton
Ed Hitchens
Jay Jones
Richard Leon
Adam Mohr
Dale Mohr
Tim Mohr
Chris Munoz
Mark Ouellette
Lawrence Pinay
Ron Ross
Shaun St. Jean
Alvin Sentes
Larry Sentes
Mike Schmegelski
Curt Seib
Gord Seib
Brad Sereda
Dean Stachoski
Aaron Stang
Joe Sylvester
Peter Theriault
Randy Wagner
Jody Wilde

## BRODA CONSTRUCTION

Jonathon Anderson
Gary Acorn
Dana Anderson
Dustin Anderson
Keith Bacon
Brian Balan
Mike Balan
Darrell Baraniecki
Dwain Barisoff
William Beavereye
James Bennett
Brett Bertram
Kevin Bird
Arthur Bishop
Norm Blunt
Bruce Boehm
Dwight Bonderud
Bob Boyer
Don Boyer
Cas Broda
Gordie Broda
Rob Broda
Jim Broderick
Mike Buness
Dale Brown
Darcy Brown
Sherry Brown
Dale Bruce
Delaney Bruce
Terry Bruce
Barry Buck
Troy Carlson
Guy Carrier
Jerry Chermcora
Larry Chorneyko
Darwin Chubey
Walter Chubey
Donnie Chupa
Jayson Clunie
Russ Clunie Jr.
Mark Davies
Deon Debussac
Travis Deforest
Trent Deforest
Jason Diewold
Lyle Ellis
Jeremy Englot
Jeremy Fatteicher
Andy Featherling
Len Fehr
John Ferniuk
Ben Fitzgerald
Joe Fitzgerald
Michael Fitzgerald
Shawn Fletcher
Warren Foord
Dale Fraser
David Fraser
Garrett Fraser
Robert Fredin
Elliot Gale
Roger Gale
Garrett Cowan
Matt Giesbrecht
Brent Gnyp
Bernie Goertzen
Jeff Goertzen
Art Gray
Ed Guest
Bruce Hamilton
Elvin Harder
Tim Harris
Chris Harwood
Rudy Hausermann
Shawn Haus
Robert Hellegards
Clifton Herman
Ted Holobetz
Clinton Hoppe
Terry Hoppe
Dan Hudye
Murry Hunter
Clarence Hupet
Len Istace
Calvin Jaman
Jason Jaman
Darren Jansen
John Johnson
Denny Jorgenson
Walter Kazakoff
Don Keir
Ed Kerluke
Dennis Kotylak
Harvey Kovac
Boris Kowalyshen
Dwayne Kruk
Todd Kulczycki
Stacey Kun
Wes Lafontaine
Glen Lamb
Jack Langford
Trenton Leis
Don Lewis
Devon Linfitt
Matthew Linfitt
Carl Lipp
Terry Lubkiwski
Rory Mann
Shaun Maurer
Daniel McCannon
Jock McDonald
Ron McLeod
Pat Morgan
Geoffrey Myles
Jamie Nagy
Colin Njaa
Don Njaa
Bernard Nokinsky
Gordie Olexyn
Eric Paproski
Ken Paproski
Kurt Paproski
Ed Pearson
Todd Pedwerbeski
Darrell Perlitz
Larry Peshke
Grant Peterson
Jordan Peterson
Dwayne Pfeifer
Andy Popoff
Dwayne Popoff
Rod Ratcliffe
Greg Reeder
Dwight Remezoff
Daniel Rezansoff
Jean Mark Robichaud

# MANPOWER

## Broda Employees

Mike Romaniuk
Robert Romaniuk
Darcy Ross
Russ Clunie, Sr.
Les Schiffo
Ryan Semeschuk
Nick Sendecki
Bob Shore

Curtis Simmonds
Lorne Sommerfelt
Chad Stajniak
Martin Stajniak
Brian Steward
Mike Stratychuk
Ron Sushelnitski
Shaun Szostak

John Szpakowski
Roger Trudeau
Jason Trudel
Ron Wakefield
Gary Wason
Dan Wartmann
Robert Watkins
Mike Wiederspick

Bruce Williams
Bruce Wilson
David Wojcichowsky
William Zatwarniski
Blake Zielinski

## Women involved in the dig:

Sherry Brown, office administrator and safety co-ordinator for the Broda operations.
Lana Wilder was Clifton's safety officer.
Broda, Dominion and Clifton had many women on their administrative support staff.

# CHALLENGES

### Weather

The 24/7 operation was shut down three times by snowstorms which made it impossible to see the haul road. January brought bitterly cold temperatures dipping down to -55 C.
Ice fog blanketed Regina early January 29.
Work shut down when Regina was struck by first blizzard of the year on January 30.
Blowing snow and visibility problems – February 10.
Warm weather caused a sticky lake bed causing productivity slowdown – February 24.
As the dig was in the home stretch, the third week in March, it rained.

## COST BREAKDOWN

$18-million budget

Federal contribution $9 million, province $5 million and the City of Regina $4 million

## HISTORY OF WASCANA LAKE

On May 24, 1884, the Queen's birthday was celebrated by the first of many boat races on Wascana Lake. That same year a scow was launched and residents paid a small fee for "a trip by water that was a welcome change from dusty prairie trails."

In the early 1900s, Wascana Lake was a reservoir fed by Wascana Creek. Reginans used the water for domestic use and livestock watering. In 1908 the reservoir was deepened to create an artificial lake which could be used for recreation and irrigation of the new legislative grounds. Years after the First World War, a sternwheeler named Queen Mary took people on lake voyages for 15 cents.

In 1931, Wascana Lake was drained, deepened again and enlarged. Excavated soil was used to form Willow and Spruce Islands. In 1956, the lake's eastern portion was declared a Federal Migratory Bird Sanctuary. In the 1970s and '80s, boating and rowing were established on Wascana Lake. In the 1990s, Dragon Boat racing began on Wascana Lake. Prior to the new millennium, Wascana Lake gradually filled with sediment to the point where the average depth was only 1.5 metres. By 2003, 35 per cent of the lake depth had been lost.

*Looking toward the City and University of Regina from Wascana Country Club, this new hill is a legacy of the excavated soil from The Big Dig*

photo by Roy Antal

# 1931 Dig – Facts & Figures

Work started Tuesday, Sept. 8, 1931

Superintendent/foreman of work was Beatty Beaubier

The project provided employment for 2,107 people.

The Department of Public Works was responsible for deepening Wascana Lake by about two feet. The project also resulted in the construction of two islands.

Men employed on the 1931 Big Dig were nominated through the Relief Department of the City of Regina.

The first contingent of the Wascana Lake Relief gang numbered 100 men equipped with shovels, picks, dump wagons and teams. They started Regina's first major relief project – the deepening of Wascana Lake, early Tuesday morning on September 8, 1931. On Saturday an advance shift of 33 men started preparing a road to the proposed island site so the wagons had no difficulty in removing the earth. Dump wagons were scarce in Regina because of contracts awarded by the Department of Highways for approximately 700 miles of road work outside the city. Approximately 20 ordinary wagons were rebuilt to make them suitable for use on the project and 12 wagons were shipped in from Maple Creek. According to a September 4, 1931 letter from James F. Bryant, Minister of Public Works, to the City Commissioner, a shift of two men worked from 6 a.m. until 12:30 p.m. with a half hour lunch. A second shift of men worked from 12:30 to 7 p.m.

Wages were 40 cents per hour. Men were paid by cheque so they could "pay their rent and taxes and buy clothing and school books, in addition to buying their food and fuel. All work is to be done by hand labour."

The earth was shovelled by hand into dump wagons. The dump wagons, probably three to a team of horses, carried the earth to the island. Sixty cents per hour was suggested as pay for a man and team "but it may be possible that will have to be increased owing to the fact that the teams will be worked on a six hour shift per day." The Government paid $3 per yard to district farmers to supply stones for the sloping sides of the islands.

On September 14, 1931, 54 wagons were at work and organizers hoped that number would increase to 92 by the middle of the week. Although wagons were in short supply, the hope was that 125 wagons would be procured to provide labour for 800 to 1,000 men per day.

## A day in the life of the 1931 Wascana Lake Improvement Project
### September 12

### Morning Shift

128 labourers @ 40 cents an hour for 768 hours = $307.20
29 teams @ 70 cents an hour for 174 hours = $121.80
1 time keeper = $4
2 straw-bosses @ $2.75 per shift = $5.50
35 wagons @ 50 cents an hour = $17.50
929 yards for a.m. shift

### Afternoon Shift

129 labourers @ 40 cents an hour for 774 hours = $309.60
31 teams @ 70 cents an hour = $130.20
1 timekeeper = $4
2 straw-bosses @ $2.75 per shift = $5.50
42 wagons @ 50 cents an hour = $21
971 yards for afternoon shift

## List of Surplus Material from 1931 Dig:

| | | |
|---|---|---|
| 33 clamps & bolts for waggons | 4 short shovels | 3 logging chains |
| 3 oil cans | 2 waggon jacks | 1 monkey wrench 15 inch |
| 179 long handle shovels | 8 complete picks | 1 P.B. hammer |
| 24 eveners | 1 pick handle | 1 claw hammer |
| 7 waggon wrenches | 5 rakes | 1 brace |
| 7 clevises | 5 hip rubbers | 1/2 keg 4-inch spikes |
| 4 sets double trees & wiffle trees | 1 – 45 gallon water tank | 95 yards rip-rap |
| 38 wiffle trees | 8 waggon keys | 40 boxes |
| 5 dippers | 1 saw | Shacks – toilets |
| 3 pails | 1 sledge hammer | |

## Total Yardage – Wascana lake 1931 Dig

Boat landing – 624 yards

Bank improvement – 5,981.6 yards

Island No. 1 – 44446.2 yards

Island No. 2 – 43478.7 yards

N.E. corner Albert Street Bridge – 804.6 yards

Fill Bay north of Broad Street Bridge – 1833.3 yards

Dirt Fill into Trees – 943.2 yards

S.E. corner Broad Street Bridge – 1421.3 yards

Paddling Pool – 448 yards

Borrow Pit Fill at foot of riprap – 7,920 yards

Bank improvement blade grader (into creek) – 1,200 yards

Total yardage Wascana Creek – 109,100.9 yards


Information courtesy of City of Regina Archives – COR 19-146

*It comes full circle – a year of activity in the new Wascana Centre*

photos by Roy Antal

↑ pic of Cooper - was almost cover photo

*Preparing for winter 2004 – Wascana Centre employees Lynette Smith and Garth Horsman prepare the fountain at Trafalger Outlook for removal for the winter*

# Biography

Bob Hughes' love affair with Wascana Centre began when he was a child. From his birth in Regina, he visited Wascana Lake with his parents. His father, known as Sailor Bob, was a rower with the Regina Rowing Club and weekends and evenings were often spent in the clubhouse in Wascana Park.

Hughes has never really stopped visiting Wascana Centre and when The Big Dig took place in the winter of 2004, he was there on an almost daily basis. Fascinated by what he described in his *Leader-Post* column as "the biggest single project the City of Regina has ever been involved in," he jumped at the chance to write a book on The Big Dig and on the history of Wascana Centre.

Hughes joined the *Leader-Post* as a copy boy in 1962 and has served in virtually every capacity with the newspaper during his long career. After a nearly 20-year career as a sports writer and columnist, Hughes moved into management,

*photo by Roy Antal*
*Bob Hughes*

becoming Managing Editor of the paper in 1988. In 1993, at the age of 48, he was the youngest person ever to be appointed Publisher of the newspaper. He also has been Editor-In-Chief of the *Leader-Post* and is currently the newspaper's Executive Editor. Hughes writes a daily column that appears on Page 2 of the paper. Hughes also is well known as an after-dinner speaker, having attended dinners throughout Saskatchewan, Alberta and British Columbia. He has worked as a commentator in both radio and television.

Hughes was awarded a Canada 125 medal by the Governor-General of Canada for his community work and also has been named to the Canadian Football League's Hall of Fame, Football Reports of Canada section.

*The Big Dig* is Hughes' second book. In 2003, he wrote *Regina Rams – A Winning Tradition*, a history of the Regina Rams football club.

## TO ORDER ADDITIONAL COPIES OF:

# THE BIG DIG
### THE MIRACLE OF WASCANA CENTRE

$19.95 (plus shipping and G.S.T.)
Total per book $25.63

Please contact:

Centax Books and Distribution
1150 Eighth Avenue
Regina, Saskatchewan
Canada  S4R 1C9
Phone: 306-359-7580
FAX: 306-359-6443

E-mail: centax@printwest.com
www.centaxbooks.com